Andrew Yeoh and Juanita Cheung
Photographs by Ching Ping Lau

Hong Kong

A guide to recent architecture

••• ellipsis KÖNEMANN

•••

CREATED, EDITED AND DESIGNED BY
Ellipsis London Limited
55 Charlotte Road London EC2A 3QT
E MAIL ...@ellipsis.co.uk
WWW http://www.ellipsis.co.uk
PUBLISHED IN THE UK AND AFRICA BY
Ellipsis London Limited
SERIES EDITOR Tom Neville
EDITOR Annie Bridges
SERIES DESIGN Jonathan Moberly
LAYOUT Pauline Harrison

COPYRIGHT © 1998 Könemann
Verlagsgesellschaft mbH
Bonner Str. 126, D-50968 Köln
PRODUCTION MANAGER Detlev Schaper
PRINTING AND BINDING Sing Cheong
Printing Ltd
Printed in Hong Kong

ISBN 3 8290 0471 0 (Könemann)
ISBN 1 899858 61 X (Ellipsis)

Andrew Yeoh and Juanita Cheung 1998

Hong Kong

...

A guide to recent architecture

Tables 88

This restaurant is housed in the old Stanley police station which was originally built in 1859. One of the oldest colonial buildings still in existence in Hong Kong, it is one of only 30 buildings protected under the Antiquities and Monuments Ordinance. A posting to the Stanley police station was considered unhealthy, isolated and fraught with danger, mainly because of a serious piracy problem. These problems got worse and by the 1850s Stanley was all but abandoned except for 28 hectares on the Stanley peninsula reserved for army artillery practice.

Later, in the early part of this century, the area became a popular seaside village, and still has a unique feel to it. Walk past the so-called bargains of Stanley Market and look at the strip of buildings facing the sea. Despite some rather unattractive attempts to tart them up, several of the buildings still have a faded-seaside-resort glamour to them, which is appealing in a melancholic, dreamy sort of way.

The white-painted exterior of the restaurant feels clean, stark and utilitarian – in complete contrast to its dark interior which has a slightly secretive atmosphere. Someone's imagination has run riot here: the place looks as if it has been designed by a person in the grip of a tropical fever. The concept – a 'living museum' – plays on the building's historical character but, unlike in a museum where attempts are made to categorise and order its displays, here the various features clash wildly in a seemingly chaotic fashion. Outside, a neat and proper row of potted palm trees swaying gently in the occasional breeze is misleading and belies the turmoil within.

After passing through an artificially lit cave-like entrance, you arrive at the Atrium bar. The place screams Bedrock with its stone walls and chunky wooden furniture (bird's-eye burlwood). And on the chair backs, twigs protrude from behind dark-indigo batik-print upholstery. Beautiful old wide-planked floorboards are used throughout. All the timber is

Roymann Design Ltd 1988

Roymann Design Ltd 1988

either salvaged (mostly from a redundant 120-year-old factory in Chicago), found wood or driftwood. It is almost a 1950s-cocktail-lounge idea of exotica (and not necessarily Asian – could we be deep in the jungles of Peru?). Bright daylight filters through wavy, oxidised steel 'branches' extending from tree-trunk columns. The irregular patterns of light made by all the objects in the space give it a heady and dramatic atmosphere.

A series of theme rooms follows and continues on to the first floor, where styles change drastically from one room to the next. Although confusing and difficult to read, this is somehow effective. It does feel as if any dinner here would be an event. There are numerous symbolic elements in the decor but none of them easy to decipher. If this were a space in a virtual computer game, you would no doubt double-click on them to reveal a secret passageway. The washrooms with their carved-out stone basins are even more Flintstoney. Incidentally, even the presentation of our chocolate dessert (the food is dubbed 'cuisine sauvage' and 'mondo cuisine') matched the chairs we were sitting on: thin chocolate twigs propped up to form a canopy over a squashy, dark mousse form. To complete the adventure, a glass cabinet displays a collection of Tables 88 souvenirs for sale. JC

Aberdeen and Stanley

ADDRESS 88 Stanley Village Road
BUSES 6, 260 to Stanley
ACCESS open

Roymann Design Ltd 1988

Roymann Design Ltd 1988

Ocean Park

Ocean Park, opened in 1977, is the world's largest oceanarium and one of the most diverse recreational and educational complexes in Asia. Developed by the Royal Hong Kong Jockey Club on land granted free by the government, it covers a total of some 87 hectares. Spanning a high, rocky peninsula between Aberdeen and Deep Water Bay, the lowland and headland sites are linked by cable car. At the headland, the 4000-seat Ocean Theatre features daily performances by trained dolphins and sea lions. A simulated rocky coastline and an artificial atoll recreating the shallows and depths of a tropical coral reef are visible from viewing galleries on four levels. On display in the four-storey-deep aquarium are some 300 species of marine life. There is also a garden theatre, a zoo, aviary, butterfly house, children's playground, goldfish exhibition and many other attractions.

In 1985 Ocean Park was expanded to include active recreational facilities, and access to the park was improved by the creation of a second entrance through a series of outdoor escalators on the mountainside bordering Tai Shu Wan. In the headland area, six major rides, including one of the world's longest and fastest rollercoasters, offer new excitement for the adventurous, and the original lake and pools in the lowland area have been redeveloped to form Asia's first aquatic play-park, Water World, complete with giant slides, a rapids ride and a variety of pools.

In Middle Kingdom, completed in 1989, 13 dynasties and 5000 years of China's history are unfolded through replica buildings, theatre and street shows, and arts and crafts demonstrations. AY

LOCATION Ocean Park Road, Aberdeen
MTR Island Line, Admiralty Station
ACCESS open

Wong Tung and Partners Ltd 1977–

Aberdeen and Stanley

Wong Tung and Partners Ltd 1977–

North Point and
Tai Koo Shing

K Wah Centre

This building is basically a large interesting object. Its entrance is mundane – a sort of postmodern/art deco job – and the floorplans above unremarkable. But from far away, and ideally without the much-sought-after 'sense of scale', it becomes fascinating. It looks like a rectangular box caught in the act of morphing into a cylinder. It could be a contemplative piece, forcing your mind to waver between two readings – is it more rectangular or more cylindrical? The same square grid of reflective turquoise glazing is used throughout, giving the building the unreal appearance of a CAD wire-frame model. It is also a game of geometry. Look at the intersecting planes. Gaps in one form reveal parts of another. What do the residual spaces look like? Then again, some people think it looks like a skull. JC

North Point and Tai Koo Shing

ADDRESS 191 Java Road
MTR North Point
ACCESS open

Simon Kwan

Simon Kwan

Kodak House

This is the home of Kodak (Far East) as well as the Hong Kong branch of Eastman Chemical Ltd. The spectacularly large red Kodak logo at the top of the building makes this glaringly obvious, but there are other clues to its occupant's line of work. From the raised superhighway that speeds past, it is an ordinary box-shaped building except for the first few floors at the back where the car park juts out. The curved corners make this part of the building look like the back of an open camera. The walls resemble the shape of film when it is drawn out of its canister and wound across to the other side.

The building is clad in highly polished square tiles, mainly in a dusty pink colour, and interesting patterns are formed by the tiles and the windows. The patterns are mainly abstract (or cryptic) stripes and squares, but if you look carefully at one group of squares you will notice a series of little grey squares above a series of much larger grey rectangles. This looks like film! The smaller squares are the sprocket holes and the larger rectangles are the images.

A corner entrance has stone steps and traditional stone carvings salvaged from the previous building on the site. JC

North Point and Tai Koo Shing

ADDRESS 321 Java Road
MTR North Point
ACCESS open

Spence Robinson Architects 1992

North Point and Tai Koo Shing

Spence Robinson Architects 1992

Hong Kong Island eastern corridor

Before this expressway was built, the only route connecting the densely populated Eastern district (population 500,000) with the central areas of Hong Kong Island was King's Road. Not surprisingly, this was the most congested thoroughfare in Hong Kong. Unfortunately the areas it passed and connected were so built up that there was no room for a new road. It was finally decided that the only solution was to build where no buildings yet existed – in the harbour. The spectacular 9-kilometre six-lane superhighway now shoots past the North Point waterfront, connecting the Eastern district with Causeway Bay and Central. The most expensive section to build was the first stage, a 3.7-kilometre stretch between Causeway Bay and Tai Koo Shing, as it was either on elevated structures over water or at ground level on reclaimed land.

The trouble with this piece of architecture is that because its *raison d'être* is to speed you along at a record-breaking rate, it is quite difficult to get a good look at it. But if you go on foot to North Point, to the car park of the K Wah building, you can get a close-up of the huge monolithic pillar supports rising out of the water. The sheer scale of these structures is breathtaking and you can feel the desperation that led to the expressway's excessive bulk. It now takes less than five minutes from Causeway Bay to Tai Koo Shing, and travelling time from Central to Shau Kei Wan has been reduced to only 20 minutes.

At the opening of the corridor, 80,000 people walked along it in a special traffic-free charity event which raised some HK$1 million. JC

North Point and Tai Koo Shing

ACCESS no pedestrian access

Hong Kong Government Highways Department mid 1980s

Hong Kong Government Highways Department mid 1980s

Coffee Culture

The Quarry Bay area was previously planned for industry, but much of this has now moved to China, leaving vacant factories and old buildings less than 15 storeys high (low-rise for Hong Kong). One of the first of a new wave of clubs, cafés and restaurants to enter the area, Coffee Culture also represents a new breed of place styled and frequented by a younger generation of Hong Kongers. It is in a hybrid style – a mixture of Japanese kitsch and 1950s Hong Kong with a bit of 1980s Europop thrown in – that has already influenced graphic design and fashion.

The coffee bar is not a place for lounging around in ('Greek style') as per the original misconstrued brief, but rather somewhere for a quick break and caffeine-fix for the young, got-to-motor crowd. The energetic design uses colour excellently: it soothes (ice-cream pastels) and revives (bright lights and chrome) at the same time. The terrazzo floor is particularly beautiful with multicoloured pieces of solid and glass aggregate. A fully glazed sidewall can be opened up to allow tables to spill outside when necessary (probably quite often as everything from washrooms to preparation areas, storage, and dining hall had to fit into the 38-square-metre interior). Furniture also uses space cleverly: hollow spaces underneath the glass-topped tables and bars are filled with products and a display of art work, creating a mini gallery under your coffee cup.

A very refreshing space, proving that a tight budget and limited space are no excuse for a lack of inventiveness. JC

ADDRESS Tong Chong Street, Quarry Bay
SIZE 38 square metres
MTR Quarry Bay or Tai Koo
ACCESS open

architect and date unknown

North Point and Tai Koo Shing

architect and date unknown

Tai Koo Shing

Take the MTR island line, get off at Tai Koo station and you enter one of Hong Kong's densest private housing estates. The scale of the construction is so large that it is possible to live, work and play here without ever leaving the complex. The site covers a total area of 21.4 hectares in the north-east quadrant of Hong Kong Island and was originally a dockyard for the repair of ships. In 1972, after the need for such a facility had declined, Swire Properties Ltd proposed a redevelopment scheme to create a new residential community, together with a shopping and entertainment centre.

From the MTR dual direction platform, escalators lead up to the station concourse. For structural reasons, Tai Koo station has a unique barrel-vault structure to achieve its 30-metre column-free span. The concrete ceiling is boldly exposed. With access provided at both ends, the structure gives exceptional clarity to a busy public space. Services are partly hidden by a suspended ceiling which runs the full length of the tunnel. The station itself also acts as a tunnel link between different phases of the Tai Koo Shing and other housing complexes.

Follow the signs to Tai Koo Shing. Escalators bring you to the re-established ground level, widening corridors and natural daylight lead to the central atrium. This is the heart of the complex – a major commercial entertainment centre and a focal point for both community and regional activities. City Plaza contains department stores, markets, restaurants, cafés, ice-skating rinks and a bowling alley. Adjoining it are various office blocks. The centre has access to the island's eastern corridor as well as numerous public transport facilities. On three sides of the central atrium are five levels of shopping arcades, interconnected by ramps at the fourth side to facilitate disabled access. The other focal point of the complex is the indoor ice-skating rink, a generous double-height space filled with

Wong Tong & Partners 1984

North Point and Tai Koo Shing

Wong Tong & Partners 1984

large neon advertising panels. Hung from the ceiling and packed densely together, these signs form a dazzling visual complexity (which can be seen from the other end of the shopping mall), like the street scenes in the film *Blade Runner*.

The project comprises 64 residential blocks with an average height of 28 storeys. The population of just over 50,000 live in approximately 14,000 apartments. The overall site density is an astonishing seven units per 100 square metres. AY

North Point and Tai Koo Shing

ADDRESS Tai Koo Shing
CLIENT Swire Properties Limited
TOTAL GROSS FLOOR AREA 56,000 square metres
COST HK$2.6 billion
MTR Tai Koo Shing (architect YRM International)
ACCESS open

Wong Tong & Partners 1984

North Point and Tai Koo Shing

Wong Tong & Partners 1984

Sheung Wan and the Peak

Hillside escalator link

This 800-metre-long hillside escalator (the longest in the world) linking Central and Mid-Levels was built to ease traffic congestion and pressure on transport services. The 20 escalators and three travelators took two and a half years to complete, at a cost of over HK$205 million. However, one small fact has reduced its efficacy – many residents of the Mid-Levels do not consider an easier journey and reduced travel time good enough reasons to abandon their cars.

The pedestrian-moving system starts on Connaught Road and progresses past the Hang Seng Bank building and the Central Market to Queen's Road where it starts its ascent along Cochrane Street and Shelley Street, continuing all the way up to its final destination in Conduit Road. The route is covered by a curved glass roof and open at the sides to let in air and light. The full journey takes approximately 20 minutes and you are likely to witness a wide variety of Hong Kong life along the way – perhaps even a wedding in a chapel. Different segments of the escalators have been partially blocked with opaque glass to avoid turning all users into voyeurs, yet it is shockingly easy to get around this impediment by bending down and peering through the railings. This act was made immortal in Wong Kar-Wai's cult film *Chungking Express*, which explores the relationship between the private interior space of an apartment and the public space of the moving escalator. The fronts of the local antique stores are opened up to display their wares, and with 29 handy entry and exit points, you can easily hop on and off to browse. JC

LOCATION from Connaught Road (first escalator along Victoria Street)
MTR Sheung Wan
ACCESS downhill from 6.00–10.00; uphill from 10.00–22.00

Hong Kong Government Transport Department 1993

Sheung Wan and the Peak

Young Associates' office

Situated among the antique shops and retailers on Hollywood Road, a solid teak door set at an angle to the street signals the entrance to Young Associates' design practice. The office occupies the first floor of an early 1960s low-rise housing block. From across the street, glimpses of the office can be seen through the floor-to-ceiling glazing which stretches across the façade.

Concrete and plywood are materials that have been widely used in Hong Kong, but they are rarely expressed or treated as a finish. Young Associates have changed all that, as demonstrated here in their own office. Beyond the entrance, a concrete staircase leads up to the office level and all floors are of fair-faced concrete. The rough surfaces are painted with resin, a treatment which gives richness to the space. Cupboards and shelves are carefully made to subdivide the office into smaller utility areas. Particular attention has been given to the use of plywood, and the characteristics of this material have been expressed wherever possible. Movable partitions built into the furniture provide a further degree of separation, although they are more decorative than functional. The 'rough and ready' theme extends to the treatment of electrical and computer cables, which are hung casually from the ceiling.

The generous spatial arrangement of these offices, unlike most in Hong Kong, makes for a pleasant working environment. Their carefully selected materials and clean tectonic lines provide an interior in sharp contrast to the street outside. AY

ADDRESS 48 Hollywood Road
COST HK$600,000
MTR Island line, Central station/Mid-Level escalator
ACCESS limited

Young Associates 1995

Sheung Wan and the Peak

Graham Street office

This sleek office conversion is just five minutes' walk from Young Associates' own office (see previous entry). In the midst of the noise and chaos of Graham Street Market, a minimal glass wall and full-height solid teak door announce the presence of this small ground-floor property, built in the 1940s. Since the office relies heavily on computers, the architects took advantage of the generous ceiling height and raised the floor level to accommodate the mass of cables. The clear resin-painted concrete floor, made out of 1-metre-square precast panels, each with a cable access hold and a stainless-steel cover plate, gives a unifying richness and flexibility to this small-footprint office. AY

Sheung Wan and the Peak

ADDRESS 35 Graham Street
COST HK$500,000
MTR Island line, Central station/Mid-Level escalator
ACCESS limited

Young Associates 1993

Contents

Introduction

City of excess, city of contrasts, city of extremes. Everything that can be said about Hong Kong applies equally and simultaneously to its architecture. For today's multitude of observers, the built environment is the most visual expression of contemporary Hong Kong. Individual visitors to the city, usually well versed in its 'barren rock' beginnings, never fail to marvel at the remarkable scope of what has been achieved in such a short period of time. In turn, local residents have a phenomenal pride in their city's architecture, to an extent unmatched elsewhere in the world.

People here seem to have a personal, almost intimate relationship with the buildings – everyone has their likes and dislikes and there are few who do not speak passionately about them. This might be due in part to the traditional Chinese belief in *feng shui*, in which buildings are often animated with powers and people speak convincingly about one building causing another's anguish or good fortune – the most well-known case of this being the Bank of China's 'dagger-like' pointing at the former residence of the Governor of Hong Kong. Most probably, however, the special relationship which exists here between people and buildings arises from the lack of natural landmarks and the desperate need to find a sense of identity – something which has been continuously and unrelentingly questioned over the last few decades. The architecture has provided a tangible source of attachment, symbolising both the singularity of the city and, perhaps, the greater and contentious issues of democracy and freedom. It remains an undeniable fact that expats scattered around the world become quite emotionally charged at the sight of a recent image of the ever-changing skyline back home.

It is this skyline – one of the most, if not *the* most, exciting of all skylines existing today – which is explored in this guide and broken up into individual projects. Unlike in other major cities, here the buildings are for the most part concentrated in one area and accessible even to those with only a few jet-lagged hours to spare. Hong Kong is the quintessential city-that-never-sleeps and it is possible to explore its well-lit architecture even by night. Since the early 1980s, major developments have started to move out of the central areas but, even so, it is still possible to see most of them while adopting the local Hong Kong attitude of refusing to venture too far.

This guide is not intended to be an inventory of architecture from this recent period in the city's development but, rather, a representative selection of projects which capture the present mood. The selection is personal and although it aims to deviate from that of the numerous coffee-table volumes on Hong Kong, it does include 'must-see' buildings. We hope that these entries will not only provide a basic knowledge about these projects (many of which may already be familiar), but also provoke hearty and vigorous debate. As with the present political climate in Hong Kong, ongoing open discussion at an international level is imperative if the city's architecture is to continue to flourish.

A cross-section of projects from Central district has been included to illustrate the fluidity of form which characterises Hong Kong. One of the first things one usually notices about this city is how its architecture seems to be a continuum of overlapping structures, often perceived as a blur rather than as isolated individual projects. This guide therefore can be seen as a freeze-frame at the time of the changeover from British to Chinese rule – both to still this blur and to capture a fleeting moment. However, within this short time-frame, it is interesting to note that there are some projects whose life-span has been too brief to register in this snapshot – for instance, the transient Vietnamese Refugees' School (Chan and Chan Architects), a fascinating piece of architecture in which an arrangement of ordinary cargo containers was used to house desperately

Hong Kong: a guide to recent architecture

needed classrooms. Hong Kong has always been a sell-by-dated city and, because of this, buildings do not need to last. Hong Kong does not ask this of its structures – and perhaps this accounts for the diversity which arises. Buildings only have to have meaning for the present. The strong 'go for broke' feeling of the last two decades gained considerable momentum as Hong Kong hurtled towards the end of its lease. The generally conservative attitude of Hong Kong society now seems at odds with the level of innovation in the architecture.

There are many other examples of contrasts and unexpected partnerships in the architecture of this city. For instance, the hard-nosed business capital where crisp tailored suits make imperative and pragmatic decisions throughout the day is also the city where spirits are around every corner, where evil ones are placated by incense and diverted by the careful placement of mirrors, chimes or 'sharp corners', where construction can grind to a halt if workers suspect mischievous ghosts are lurking in the scaffolding. The dense, slick, high technology to be found in the structures of Central is seemingly sewn together by elements such as bamboo scaffolding, illegal façades and ad hoc alleyways.

As in other built-up cities, the architecture here exists in layers and at different scales which often need to be read separately. Large commercial projects are all geared to the view from the harbour; consequently, behind the first visible vertical layer, the design of subsequent layers of buildings suffers from a 'top-obsessed' syndrome. What seems to matter most (after the lettable square footage has been calculated) is just how prominent the crown of the building is – together with the visibility of the name or logo of the main client. The entrance may be on another façade, but a building will always face the harbour. A secondary point of polarity on Hong Kong Island is Victoria Peak, but this is more like a slight nod of acknowledgement to someone backstage – the real audience is out front. Some buildings sporting deceptively enticing headgear in an attempt to grab attention turn out to be insignificant pieces of architecture and disappoint up close. In many cases, the main bulk of a building and its party-hat top simply do not relate at all; they may even possess conflicting elements.

Another entirely different atmosphere exists at street level – all three or four of them. In some of the narrower streets, or perhaps those with a congestion of street signs above, the top of the building becomes completely insignificant. Often lobbies exist in their own right – some, mammoth constructions on an altogether different sense of scale, have their own little summits. The much-used so-called podium levels further divide tall buildings into multiple personalities. Raised pedestrian walkways, buildings on sloped sites (especially in Central), and the underground levels of the MTR, make for an architecture that is far more three-dimensional. This perception is heightened by the use of indoor/outdoor escalators which cut diagonally between the levels. The actual ground level becomes almost irrelevant; walk-by trade for local retail businesses is not limited to this level alone and directions are given not only in rights and lefts but also in ups and downs. It is surprising then to see vast atrium spaces (at Times Square Plaza, for example) which are often larger than the voids found between buildings in real open spaces. In contemporary culture these must certainly be the modern equivalent of the enormous caves of ancient mythical worlds.

Other cities, notably in south-east Asia, are anxiously awaiting the outcome of Hong Kong's changeover. In fact, even within China itself, the late Deng Xiao Ping had envisioned a series of mini Hong Kongs, the most prominent of which was Hainan Island, complete with copycat skyscrapers. This turned out to be less than successful, and a terrible recession resulted in the departure of 200,000 people during 1996 and 1997. It was also proof of the absurdity of trying to clone Hong Kong.

Much has been said about the vertical expansion of Hong Kong, but its conventional horizontal expansion should not be ignored. The areas covered in this guide span across the whole SAR (Special Administrative Region) and it is essential that the architectural differences between these areas are recognised. The swift changes in Hong Kong industry – notably the shifting of much of the manufacturing industry to cross-border locations in the Pearl River delta and beyond in other parts of south China – have resulted in sustained growth of investment, by both private developers and the government, in a broad range of building types and infrastructure facilities. This is in order to not only provide the necessary new technology and services industries but also to promote the acceleration in allied activities, both professional and academic. Rapid urban development schemes in the satellite towns of the New Territories have only been made possible through the use of standard designs for housing and accompanying community facilities such as schools, police stations and clinics. These developments cannot be appreciated using the same criteria used for judging, say, the individual landmark buildings of the metropolitan areas on Hong Kong Island. Their design strategies, for instance, are often concerned with more subtle objectives, such as the safety, comfort and convenience of the large volumes of pedestrian traffic in their squares and covered malls.

The formation of certain areas of reclamation around Victoria Harbour is currently under way, with a planned total area of 410 hectares. New port-related reclamations for container terminals and back-up facilities are covered under the Port Development Plan and Programme. The new Chek Lap Kok Airport on Lantau Island, scheduled to open in April

1998, will replace the existing Kai Tak International Airport which will, in turn, be replaced by … a mall! A large shopping complex has been designed to occupy the vacated space and – as if this were not enough – there will be further land reclamation to fill in the gaps between the runways which currently jut out into the sea. In a dramatic domino-effect, large parts of Kowloon will immediately shoot up past the current airport height restrictions.

Of course the single most important recent event affecting Hong Kong has been the handover of power to China at midnight on 30 June 1997. The changeover did not end the uncertainty, but at least it put a stop to the frenetic, almost blinkered rush that led up to this momentous event. Perhaps Hong Kong can then pause or, rather, momentarily slow down the pace of things. Let us hope that the city will be left alone for a period of reflection. Writing on the eve of the handover, a strange thought occurs: if the many people who continue to apply for foreign passports (to ensure a safe exit if the unimaginable should happen) were to leave, they would be leaving behind those true 'citizens' of Hong Kong who cannot leave – the buildings. They will remain as a testament to the people who created them.

The architecture of Hong Kong will undoubtedly change, but then it always has. Hong Kong thrives on the energy of renewal, like a snake shedding its skin. In this new era the only real danger is the possibility that this change might not be allowed to happen.

Hong Kong: a guide to recent architecture

How to use this book

The city is divided into three geographical areas: Hong Kong Island, Kowloon peninsular and the New Territories. The nearest MTR station or appropriate public transport is listed below each entry. The Mass Transit Railway is extremely efficient, carrying more than two million people a day. The MTR is made up of three interconnecting lines: the Island line (blue), the Tsuen Wan line (red), and the Kwun Tong line (green). The Kwun Tong line links with the Kowloon-Canton Railway (KCR), which goes through the New Territories to China. Interchanges are straightforward. Most of the entries in this guide can be reached via the MTR and KCR. MTR maps are available at any MTR station ticket office.

The Star Ferry, running between Hong Kong Island and Kowloon, is among the most famous ferries in the world. It is perhaps the best introduction to this city-state's architecture and giant neon signs. In addition, there is the sheer beauty of the harbour, stunning vistas and the tranquillity of the surrounding hillsides. The ferry leaves from Wan Chai and Central on the island side, and from Hung Hom and Tsim Sha Tsui on the Kowloon side. Double-decker wooden trams are exclusive to the island. They run along what were once waterfront roads but which now, due to reclamation, are further inland. The routes run east–west along the northern side of the island facing Kowloon. The trams are slow, but offer a good view of the city.

So that you can appreciate the multiplicity of the central area, the first ten entries of Central district form a linear route, beginning at MTR Central station. It then passes through Landmark atrium to the Hongkong and Shanghai Bank, past the Bank of China tower, through the aviary in Hong Kong Park to Pacific Place and then on to the Peak Tram concourse. The Peak Tram will take you up the steep incline from Central to the top of Victoria Peak.

Taxis in Hong Kong are red and have a roof sign that lights up when available for hire. They are difficult to find between 15.30 and 18.00. Surcharges for passing through underground tunnels vary between different areas. Most taxi drivers speak some English, but to avoid problems it is best to have your destination written out in both Chinese and English.

Street signs have English as well as Chinese names, which will probably be changed rapidly after June 1997. Street maps are useful and can be obtained in most newsagents in Central.

ACKNOWLEDGEMENTS
There are many people who have helped and encouraged the writing of this book, but I would especially like to thank Chan Hung Yu, Joanna Tang, Lau Ching Ping, my patient partners Raymond and Beng Kian, and, of course, David. This book is dedicated to Matilda and Kenneth Cheung who taught me both the importance and delight of thinking critically.
JC

Thank you to Sam Holyoak, Erika Pilling, Anna Ho, and Richard Anthony Hay for their time and their enthusiasm; to Alan and Cecilia Yeoh for their encouragement. And to Tom Neville for his patience and openness to our ideas.
AY

Hong Kong: a guide to recent architecture

Aberdeen and Stanley

Repulse Bay apartments

This late-1980s attempt at Miami art deco was built to replace the famous British colonial-style Repulse Bay Hotel which opened in the 1920s. The original hotel was a prominent landmark, home to many visiting celebrities and a venue for various social events. It was known for its late-afternoon teas taken on the external verandah, and was often used as a film location. The hotel was also the last stronghold against the Japanese invasion during the Second World War, and later on was used as a hospital and recuperation centre.

Strangely enough, the new scheme includes a complete reconstruction of the former hotel – in an attempt to 'recreate the charm of the original' – though this seems to be rather overdoing nostalgia for the colonial past. The replica is a commercial complex and one of three new parts in the current project. Its 5600 square metres contain a range of shops and boutiques, a supermarket, a medical and dental clinic, and a host of other service trades. Directly behind are four apartment towers containing 209 luxury apartments and duplexes (all with panoramic views of the South China Sea) and with a total floor area of 46,500 square metres. Rents are among the highest in Hong Kong and the majority of residents are American or European expatriate employees. The residents' club (a 5570-square-metre clubhouse with recreational facilities) and car park are at the back.

The apartment towers form the main visual focus. Their undulating curvilinear façade gives the otherwise rectangular series of structures an appealing sense of fluidity, appearing to flow from right to left and ending in a 180-degree curved detail which curls back like the cap of a wave. The predominant colours are light blues with cream, peach and pink, and there are details in other ice-cream shades. However, the vigour and excitement of real Miami art deco are missing. The project lacks distinc-

Anthony K K Ng 1989

Anthony K K Ng 1989

tive detailing and this makes it seem chunky by comparison. (Originally, Miami buildings were predominantly white, with colour used only in the trimming. The painting of entire buildings in pastel shades came about only in the late 1970s after a drab, murky, brown-and-beige phase.) So, in actual fact, the Repulse Bay apartments have more in common with the suits of the *Miami Vice* team than the tropical deco style they probably sought to emulate.

The stepped skyline of the towers matches the silhouette of the steep hills behind. Three 'sky gardens' form gaps in the façade and give it a light, transparent feel. The focal point is, however, a massive (eight-storey-high) pink-edged square-shaped hole which has been punctured right through the structure to reveal the lush mountain greenery behind. It creates a strong visual impact and, as intended, helps to reduce the mass of the building form. JC

Aberdeen and Stanley

ADDRESS 109 Repulse Bay Road, Repulse Bay
STRUCTURAL ENGINEER KNW Architects & Engineers Ltd
BUSES 6, 6A, 61, 64, or 260 from the Central Bus Terminal
ACCESS public areas open

Anthony K K Ng 1989

Sheung Wan and the Peak

Young Associates 1993

Shun Tak Centre and Macau ferry terminal

Designed to deal with an estimated 15 million travellers a year, the Macau ferry terminal is one of the busiest international water-transport facilities in the world. It seems that behind nearly all recent large developments in Hong Kong, some kind of deal has been made between the Hong Kong government and a developer. Following one operator's dissatisfaction with the 25-year-old temporary terminal that previously stood on the site, the government agreed to allow it to be commercially developed in exchange for the construction of new off-shore piers. The complex now covers a land and sea area of 56,000 square metres and comprises three main parts: the land structure (a nine-level shopping complex and two 41-storey twin towers) and the inner and outer piers. Separated by 60-metre-wide water channels, the parts are joined only by pedestrian bridges.

The James Bond films of the 1970s were the obvious inspiration for this project. The architects apparently wanted a space station aesthetic in which the jetfoils would be space shuttles and passengers would feel as if they were entering a futuristic world where ease of travel (made possible by high-tech machinery of some sort) was part of the excitement. Believing that the architecture around you is made of complicated gadgetry somehow gives the otherwise dull routine procedures of international travel an extra kick. Whether or not you ever get to land your helicopter on the pad here is not the issue – just seeing the hydraulic aluminium helipad on the roof above makes your own little daytrip to Macau seem that much more interesting.

Unfortunately, a futuristic design always dates rather easily. The two towers are clad in dark reflective-glass curtain-walling divided by chunky, red steel-frame structures designed to match the red stripe running along-

Spence Robinson Architects 1986

Spence Robinson Architects 1986

side the jetfoils. For some reason this reminds me of an old Adidas gym bag in shiny black vinyl with red piping, a very popular item during a certain decade. This theme is continued in the ceiling of the harbour-side entrance of the Hotel Victoria. Covered with coloured cylindrical lighting fixtures, this has that classy/sleaze factor popular in discos and bars of the 1970s.

Furthermore, the two island piers are dead ringers for the off-shore island kingdoms of the baddies in the Bond films. The inner pier houses the immigration hall, waiting lounge and customs area, and at deck level there are eight hydrofoil platforms. The outer pier caters for jetfoils and larger vessels, with the top floor housing the Port Control Office of the Marine Department. JC

Sheung Wan and the Peak

ADDRESS 200 Connaught Road
CLIENT Shun Tak Centre Ltd
MECHANICAL AND ELECTRICAL ENGINEER Parsons Brinckerhoff (Asia) Ltd
CIVIL ENGINEERS Maunsell
LIGHTING Phillips Hong Kong Ltd, Derek Phillips Associates
MTR direct underground link to Sheung Wan station
ACCESS open

Spence Robinson Architects 1986

Sheung Wan and the Peak

Spence Robinson Architects 1986

Western Market renovation

The site was formerly one of Hong Kong's principal food markets. The existing Edwardian structure, built in 1906, is one of the very few historical buildings left in the inner city.

The project aimed to renovate this building and turn it into a shopping complex dealing primarily in traditional Chinese trades, with a restaurant on the top floor. The design consortium was determined to preserve the fast-disappearing local architecture and did all they could to retain the external fabric of the building.

Tao Ho's intention was to maintain both the integrity of the existing building and the traditional Chinese trades that were still active in the Western district. During the development of the design, Tao Ho himself became directly involved with the fabric traders. He learnt the way in which they operated and then applied the lesson to his design.

A nostalgic atmosphere has been successfully created, with the building faithfully restored and services subtly concealed. However, the general construction detail is disappointing: it lacks inventiveness and is firmly rooted in the past. Does preservation necessarily mean engage reverse gear? AY

Sheung Wan and the Peak

ADDRESS New Market Street
GROSS FLOOR AREA 4140 square metres
COST HK$60 million
MTR Sheung Wan
ACCESS open

Tao Ho Design Architects 1991

Sheung Wan and the Peak

Tao Ho Design Architects 1991

Li Po Chun chambers

The horizontal stripes of reflective blue-green glass and an American granite called Lake Placid Blue make this building easily recognisable from the harbour, but what really catches the eye is the symmetrical and sculptural form at its apex. Here, two mini-towers made of three floating layers continue the stripey motif, and piercing through them and extending many metres into the sky are two spindly antenna-like fixtures. The whole contraption is well illuminated at night (as are other details of the building) and is reminiscent of radio station or network logos from the 1930s. The antennae look as if they should have a blinding electric current flashing up between them with a loud crackle (or at least a moving neon image of one). This would really get the building noticed.

The relationship of the chambers to the harbour was considered very important and this is reflected in the care taken to provide good views in both directions – of the harbour from the building, and vice versa.

The main lobby is unusually located 11 metres above ground on the third floor, purposefully elevating it above the waterfront flyover. With its 11-metre-high ceiling and completely glazed external wall, the lobby can proudly boast an uninterrupted sea view. It is accessed by three long escalators, flanked on either side by a rectangular grid wall of light.

Because this 28-storey office tower sits on a relatively narrow plot (sandwiched between two other tall buildings), the middle convex part of the façade seems to billow out as if from pressure at its sides. The north and south façades are set back at the corners creating the *de rigueur* and prestigious executive corner offices.

All floors are column-free and symmetrical in plan, with a side core containing the central lobby for both the low- and high-zone lifts. There are separate zones in order to squeeze in extra marketable space on the upper floors over the low-zone lift shaft. Penthouse offices on the top two

Wong Tung & Partners Ltd 1995

Wong Tung & Partners Ltd 1995

floors have higher ceilings and their own internal staircases.

Trims, suspended canopies and other features are in fluorocarbon-coated aluminium. Openings forming horizontal recesses are incorporated into each panel of the curtain wall for emergency ventilation. As the building is located near an MTR station, the ground-floor entrance is set back to allow for the wider pavements needed to cope with the large number of pedestrians. JC

Sheung Wan and the Peak

ADDRESS 189 Des Voeux Road
SIZE 29,000 square metres
COST HK$354 million
MTR Sheung Wan
ACCESS open

Wong Tung & Partners Ltd 1995

Wong Tung & Partners Ltd 1995

Peak Club competition

This project is one of the most significant and well-known pieces of architecture in Hong Kong – a fact all the more impressive considering that it was never built. The competition, which attracted 539 entries from all around the world, was to design a club, 40 guest apartments with studios, and a residence for the promoter's own family. The jury consisted of architects John Andrews (chairman), Arata Isozaki and Gabriel Formoso, as well as Ronald Poon (director of the Hong Kong Institute of Architects) and Alfred Siu, the owner of the site and initiator of the international competition.

As the story goes, the competition's technical advisors were asked to make a preliminary selection, and 400 of the entries were eliminated. The jury was not satisfied with this and insisted on reviewing the rejected pile. From these entries Isozaki rescued Zaha Hadid's submission and nominated it for first place. The other jurors had decided on a different winner, but with the support of Alfred Siu, Isozaki convinced them of 'the uniqueness of expression and the strength of logic' of the entry, claiming 'it must win because it gives itself up to the forces inherent in style itself'.

Although Hadid was the outright winner and the ample prize money enabled her to open her London office, it was not until 1988, with the opening of 'Deconstructivist Architecture' exhibitions in New York and London, that due recognition was attributed to the project and the landmark design and competition took their place in architectural folklore.

The winning design was unusual in its interpretation of the site's relationship with the dense city below – which it overlooked. The notion of skyscrapers was reinterpreted horizontally, forming dramatic layers which would slice through the hillsides of Victoria Peak. The design called for the excavation of a mass of granite – which was to be polished and reabsorbed elsewhere on the site by the natural landscape – leaving in

Sheung Wan and the Peak

Zaha M Hadid 1982–83

Zaha M Hadid 1982–83

its place the new structure. In its creation of a new geology and architecture, this project would have mimicked the impact of Ice Age glaciers.

Drawings show the various programmes ordered into the skewed layers of the actual structures, which are often described as floating. The beams do, indeed, seem to hover over one another, leaving gaps of various sizes to house open-air facilities such as decks, terraces and a swimming pool. Access routes to the building, for both pedestrians and cars, are linked by a curved ramp to the main road. Lifts and more ramps at the entrance deck connect the various parts internally.

The project would have been situated near the highest point of the Peak, on the west side overlooking Hong Kong and Victoria Harbour. Take the Peak Tram and then continue walking in the same direction as the last segment of the tram route, follow Mount Austin Road as it veers to the right until you reach a fork in the road. Here you can mentally superimpose the dynamic drawings of the approach by ramp on to the site in front of you and dream of what could have been. JC

LOCATION Mount Austin Road, Victoria Peak
CLIENT Alfred Siu, OLS Property Development Ltd
GETTING THERE Central MTR take either the Peak Tram from below the St John's building or bus 15 from the Central Bus Terminal (every 15 minutes, 6.15–23.00)

Zaha M Hadid 1982–83

Sheung Wan and the Peak

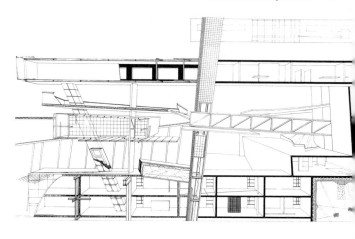

Zaha M Hadid 1982–83

The Peak Tower

In the words of one local architectural observer, Farrell was 'more inter-esting than I remembered or expected'. The Peak Tower project, which may well have been particularly significant to the British practice when design work started during the recession, is indeed more notable than his previous efforts. However, when placed in the context of its prestigious site, the tower doesn't quite fulfil expectations. The focal point of the object/building looks like a segment of an orange from the side – but not as complex in form – perched on top of four pillars between which zig-zag the fair-faced concrete and bluish-green glass stairs. An extensive viewing platform resembles an airport observation deck and offers as much protection from the summer heat and sun's glare as an airport runway.

One cannot help but wonder at the necessity of such a project. The main supporting building houses the Peak Tram terminal as well as a seemingly useless bunch of restaurants catering to the tourists who have been wandering aimlessly in the even less inspired Peak Galleria Shopping Mall across the road.

Still, the project does have its good points. The primary colours of the shiny tilework are playful and should bring a smile to visitors' faces – especially since many are of a pre-school age and appreciate that sort of thing. JC

ADDRESS 128 Peak Road, The Peak
CLIENTS Hong Kong & Shanghai Hotels Ltd/The Peak Tramway Ltd
STRUCTURAL ENGINEER Ove Arup & Partners, HK
CONTRACTOR Chung Wo
COST £14.5 million
ACCESS open

Terry Farrell & Partners 1996

Terry Farrell & Partners 1996

Illegal façades

Although many illegal façades can be found in areas such as Sham Shui Po, North Point and Pau Ma Tei (Happy Valley), there will almost certainly be at least one example not too far from wherever you happen to be standing. Just look up. You will see what is perhaps the most impressive example of Hong Kong's many varied forms of 'urban vernacular' architecture. If a single type of structure had to encapsulate what is quintessentially Hong Kong, it would have to be these unconstrained, spontaneous and anarchic expressions of the local residents rather than the giant corporate skyscrapers of the picture-postcard skyline. In fact, the sight of an unusually large example, in which the entire original façade may be obscured, is a welcome respite from the crisp slickness of Central. What the viewer sees is an organic façade, in the sense that the design has evolved and grown according to self-regulating rules. The strength of the inhabitants' belief in their constructions' ability to stay up is perhaps the only limiting factor (building regulations approval need not apply here as 'illegality' is inherent in the form). The needs and aesthetic values of each owner/builder are all that govern each individual design.

In Jerzy Wojtowicz's *Architecture – Hong Kong-Made Illegal Façades*, these structures were studied in order to find out if there were any underlying rules governing their existence and type (categorised as verandah, balcony/porch and hut). Indeed, they can be seen as a form of artificial life not unlike that described in John Conway's *Game of Life*. The likelihood of an addition or transformation happening (at any position on a given façade) can roughly be worked out by looking at the neighbouring units. If this process were speeded up (which would highlight the ever-changing status of the façades) an interesting flicker of patterns would no doubt be perceived.

Whatever you choose to read into these complex structures, they are

immensely successful as an architectural manifestation of the character of Hong Kong. At a glance, you can feel the overwhelming intensity of the residents' struggle – not only for more space but also for the recognition of their homes. The density and congestion are almost tangible as your eyes pan across these busy façades, and their image becomes imprinted on your memory. The colours, the patterns on the ornamental grillework (of some of the more cage-like spaces), the shape of awnings, the plants, and even the style of laundry line, are all expressions of the residents' creativity. The fact that these external spaces are actually open rooms of private residential properties produces a rather voyeuristic feeling in the observer, particularly when they are on the same level as pedestrian walkways. It may be precisely the kind of spirit these structures exude that will keep the future of Hong Kong vibrant under a potentially overbearing administration. JC

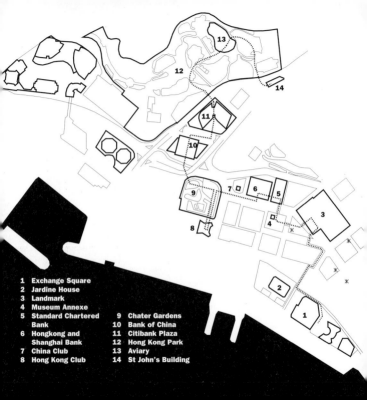

1 Exchange Square
2 Jardine House
3 Landmark
4 Museum Annexe
5 Standard Chartered
  Bank
6 Hongkong and
  Shanghai Bank
7 China Club
8 Hong Kong Club
9 Chater Gardens
10 Bank of China
11 Citibank Plaza
12 Hong Kong Park
13 Aviary
14 St John's Building

Central

Exchange Square

Home of the unified Hong Kong Stock Exchange, the Exchange Square complex (designed by Remo Riva with a team from Palmer & Turner) is one of the most popular commercial spaces in the city. Stretching across the harbour line, it comprises three phases of development and occupies a prominent position in Central district. The two office towers provide 111,500 square metres of first-class offices – currently among the most expensive rentable commercial space in Hong Kong.

The footprints of these vast buildings are composed of basic geometrical shapes. From afar, with their alternating bands of pink Spanish granite and silver reflective glass held in a prefabricated modular unit, the 52-storey towers achieve a highly polished sculptural profile. The proportions of external cladding are skilfully arranged to emphasise the distinction between the rectangular and the circular towers.

This 'architecture as sculpture' strategy has unfortunately failed to apply a more direct human scale to the complex. These buildings appear to have been designed to be looked at from a distance, as if the design process stopped at the scale of 1:100. In fact the best place to appreciate this 'sculptural form' is from the top deck of the cross-harbour ferry. From there you will see not only the articulation of the cladding but also the stepped top-floor configuration which accommodates luxury penthouses and private terraces.

With a public bus terminal occupying the whole of the ground floor, the entrance to the complex and a public plaza landscaped with water features and artworks are raised to the floor above where they connect with the central elevated walkway.

A sculpture by Henry Moore dominates the entrance area, and bronzes by Dame Elizabeth Frink and a number of large figures by Ju Ming are displayed on the outdoor plaza.

Central

P & T Architects & Engineers Ltd 1985

The main entrance lobby offers a spectacular panoramic view across the harbour to the Kowloon peninsula.

Exchange Square III is currently under construction (1997). AY

ADDRESS 8 Connaught Place
CLIENT Hong Kong Land Company Limited
SITE AREA 13,100 square metres
GROSS FLOOR AREA 213,000 square metres
COST HK$1.2 billion (Exchange Square I and II); HK$500 million (Exchange Square III)
MTR Central
ACCESS open

Central

P & T Architects & Engineers Ltd 1985

P & T Architects & Engineers Ltd 1985

Jardine House (formerly Connaught Centre)

For many years, this 52-storey structure was the tallest building in Asia. And with its distinctive façade of porthole windows it became an icon for Hong Kong during the 1970s.

When Hong Kong Land bought the site – the most expensive in the world at that time – they were anxious to produce an interesting piece of architecture as well as lettable office space. The reclaimed land created special foundation problems and the building had to be as lightweight as possible. In order to overcome these difficulties, the structure is made up of two tubes, with the perimeter walls forming an outer ring around the inner service core. This technological solution allowed for maximum flexibility and column-free office floors. To avoid reducing the strength of the outer walls, circular holes were punched through to achieve the most structurally efficient openings. Originally, the exterior was clad in Italian glass mosaics, but maintenance problems have necessitated a change to custom-made metal panels for each unique window bay. Although seemingly standardised, the slip-formed concrete façades are all slightly different due to the on-site casting method used.

A major refurbishment during 1993 gave the public area a complete facelift, after which the building became known as Jardine House. AY

ADDRESS 1 Connaught Place
CLIENT Hong Kong Land Company Limited
SITE AREA 4900 square metres
GROSS FLOOR AREA 88,000 square metres
COST HK$145 million
MTR Central
ACCESS public areas open

Central

P & T Architects & Engineers Ltd 1973

P & T Architects & Engineers Ltd 1973

Central

Landmark

From MTR Central station, exit G leads to Landmark, an early 1980s development comprising two diagonally placed 44-storey office towers (Gloucester and Edinburgh) and an enclosed plaza. The threshold is clearly defined by the station's powder-coated red panelled walls and the grey granite that marks the up-market shopping labyrinth. Follow the crowds up to the ground level where widening corridors lead to the central atrium of the building, like streets leading to a square in European cities. The atrium acts as a reference point within this enclosed environment and draws together pedestrians from different levels. The flow pattern around the atrium encourages shoppers to circulate throughout the complex.

Terraces and balconies overlook the fountain and the central space, a popular meeting place. Exhibitions, fashion shows and musical events entertain shoppers in the main lift lobby on the second floor. The escalators here also serve as the main entrance foyer to the office towers.

This high-rise office slab on a retail podium conforms to the typical configuration of commercial buildings in the Central area. A glazed pedestrian bridge which links Landmark to the Galleria across House Street is comparatively quiet, in contrast to the buzzing shopping corridors. The walk across the bridge, with its view of the city and constant traffic jams below, provides an opportunity to establish orientation with the outside world once again. AY

ADDRESS Des Voeux Road and Queen's Road
CLIENT Hong Kong Land Company Limited
GROSS FLOOR AREA 150,000 square metres
COST HK$240 million (Gloucester); HK$225 million (Edinburgh)
MTR Central
ACCESS open

P & T Architects & Engineers Ltd 1980 (phase 1), 1983 (phase 2)

P & T Architects & Engineers Ltd 1980 (phase 1), 1983 (phase 2)

Museum annexe

You can never quite predict what will be around the next corner in this ever-changing city. For example, sited among endless commercial units and tourist outlets on a dim and confined podium floor of the Prince's Building sits this bright and fresh museum annexe.

The architects have transformed a standard nondescript retail unit into a truly flexible exhibition space. It incorporates a main gallery, office area, display window, storage, and a lecture room with VDU and projection facilities, all within no more then 100 square metres of gross floor area.

Six movable panels and self-illuminating display cabinets, set on tracks and sandwiched between pockets of void for storage, are incorporated into the back wall. These can be moved and positioned anywhere in the gallery, either lined up together or pushed out to create niches at the back, or arranged at an angle for hanging displays. For further flexibility, a sliding wall panel in the blade wall can be extended to meet the structural column, subdividing the area into two distinct gallery spaces.

Also impressive are the display cabinets: like something out of a 1970s James Bond film, they are completely hidden and become part of the perimeter wall. Fitted with wheels and optional glass covers, the plinths, like everything else, offer a surprising variety of configurations.

The annexe's ability to undergo rapid spatial transformations – from gallery to shop, from lecture hall to museum – is proof that good design and attention to detail can overcome any constraints of space. AY

ADDRESS 101–102 Prince's Building
CLIENT Carol Lu
MTR Central
ACCESS open 9.00–18.00

Dr Tao Ho and Jill Cheshire 1995

The Museum Annex

Central

Dr Tao Ho and Jill Cheshire 1995

Standard Chartered Bank

Approaching the bank from The Galleria, you are ceremoniously transported from a buzzing shopping arcade into a gloomy medieval castle. This distinctive atmosphere was created by Remo Riva who, after his success with the Exchange Square complex (see page 70), chose to continue his 'buildings as sculpture' theme here at 2 Queen's Road.

The concrete tower has a lift core on the front and structural columns to one side along the perimeter. The building is meant to be perceived as a series of stone monoliths reaching for the sky. The façades of the tower facing Des Voeux Road and Queen's Road Central are set at a 45-degree angle to improve their exposure to open views. Starting at the seventeenth floor, the main façade is stepped back every six floors. This enables the building to follow the 1 to 4 angle of the shadow regulation in force at the design stage. The tower is clad in pink and beige granite – pastel tones chosen to contrast with its high-tech neighbour. The architects have tried to re-create the atmosphere of large American public banking halls of the 1930s. Kitsch motifs abound – from nasty stained-glass windows to octagonal brass ornaments.

A monumental flight of steps leads up to the main entrance, recessed from the street on a higher level. And cutting right through the centre of the foyer, a walkway elevated 10 metres over Queen's Road links the Prince's Building and the Hongkong and Shanghai Bank. The incompatibility of this building with its neighbour creates an extreme spatial and intellectual contrast. AY

ADDRESS 2 Queen's Road
COST HK$400 million
MTR Central
ACCESS banking hall open

Remo Riva and P & T Architects & Engineers Ltd 1990

Remo Riva and P & T Architects & Engineers Ltd 1990

Hongkong and Shanghai Bank

Take the internal link bridge from Standard Chartered Bank and you arrive at a high-tech icon. With its extraordinary cathedral-like atmosphere, this is no ordinary headquarters office block: it is one of the key buildings of modern architecture and a symbol of the bank's undented confidence in the future of Hong Kong. Standing at the head of Statue Square, on one of the most spectacular sites in the city, the bank overlooks a 400-metre stretch of land leading to the waterfront.

The bank's first headquarters, completed in 1886, were designed by Clement Palmer. After the Wall Street crash of 1929, the bank's chief manager commisioned Clement Palmer (of the now well-established Hong Kong practice Palmer & Turner) to design 'the best bank in the world'. But by the late 1970s the building had become outdated, unable to accommodate new banking technology. The architects of today's Hongkong and Shanghai Bank, Foster Associates, were commissioned after a 1979 international competition for the project (the six other practices competing were YRM International, Palmer & Turner, Yuncken Freeman, Hugh Stubbins, SOM and Harry Seidler Associates).

The aim of the winning scheme was to build a tower suspended over the existing banking hall so that business could continue there throughout the construction period. This tower would then be extended northwards to replace the original banking hall. The idea of hanging floor plates and 'laminated' vertical planes can still be seen on the final building.

However, although the client later ruled out the possibility of keeping any parts of the existing building other than the annexe, Foster Associates decided to retain the main features of their original design. The conventional podium-plus-central-core-tower approach for high-rise buildings was rejected. Instead, the layered space is suspended from the twin-coat-hangers structure and service cores on the edges, leaving the floors

Foster Associates 1985

Foster Associates 1985

Central

completely unobstructed.

The plaza beneath the building – providing a pedestrian route from Statue Square to Battery Park, sacrificing the traditional grand entrance and giving the space to the public – is a revolutionary concept. It is clearly visible from the galleries of the atrium through the glass underbelly that gently arcs across. High above, the internal part of the sun scoop is suspended in space, reflecting gentle sunlight on to the massive structure. The internal part of the sun scoop is static, but the external reflector is motorised and controlled by a computer to track the path of the sun.

By January 1983 the overall design was complete. Almost everything within the building was designed from scratch – handrails, benches, the glazing system and shading devices – with certain components (the air-conditioning outlet grilles) standard off-the-shelf items. During the construction period, prefabricated elements, manufactured around the world in subcontract packages, arrived on site according to tightly coordinated schedules. Collaboration with industries outside the normal sphere of the construction industry ensured rigid quality control. Mock-ups and prototypes were created to anticipate the eventual realities on site.

The building was designed to accommodate 3500 staff. More than 5000 are currently working in it. AY

ADDRESS 1 Queen's Road
CLIENT Hongkong and Shanghai Banking Corporation
GROSS FLOOR AREA 99,171 square metres
COST HK$5.2 billion
MTR Central/Mid-Level escalator
ACCESS public banking hall levels open

Central

Foster Associates 1985

Foster Associates 1985

China Club

Now completely dwarfed by its neighbours (notably the Hongkong and Shanghai Bank), the old China Bank building (1949) was originally one of the tallest in the colony. When the bank outgrew these premises, it fortunately chose to relocate rather than knock them down and rebuild.

The top three floors of the building are now home to the China Club (fees £15,000 a year), owned by the Hong Kong entrepreneur David Tang. Its interiors are modelled on the atmosphere of old Shanghai. On the first floor (and in the lobby) various artifacts – including bird cages, an old telex machine and a hat stand laden with ghostly hats – are intended to evoke the atmosphere of another more precious era. Chinese motifs feature in the steel railing to the stairs; its curved sections were made in Guangzhou then joined to Hong Kong-made flat sections.

There is something disturbing about the main themes here. A glamorisation of colonial times together with a Chinese Communist theme would seem to be quite a lethal cocktail – yet this is laughed off as tongue-in-cheek humour and ascribed to Tang's playful wit and sense of fun. Portraying the relics of repressive regimes as witty elements of interior design is at best shallow and most probably offensive to many. Perhaps the Communist theme grew out of an innocent desire to showcase the extensive collection of modern Chinese art that is on display here.

The Long March Bar, apparently designed by Tang himself, has cream walls decorated with souvenirs from Mao's rule. Just outside the bar is an original poster glorifying the Communist militia. In this long (more of the famous yet morosely untaxing wit?) and narrow space, there is barely enough room for the bar and its row of wooden stools topped with violet velvet and a single file of pale-green upholstered sofas (from Beijing's State Guesthouse). Chrome-framed prints and artwork are from the period of the Cultural Revolution. Windows (including an oversized

Leese, Robertson & Freeman 1991

Leese, Robertson & Freeman 1991

chrome 'porthole') are filled with green glass etched with horizontal stripes, and the visibly distressed wooden bar has curved mirror details and green glass panels lit from behind. Wavy, cantilevered and hinged chrome lights are copies of those seen in a Budapest café.

Other rooms are filled with old or reproduction furniture in dark wood. A group of mahogany banquettes are reminiscent of Chinese teahouses. There are pseudo art deco touches everywhere. Untraditional bright colours on the upholstery– fuchsia, yellow and green – contrast with the dark wooden furniture and floors. (Incidentally, these are the colours of the clothes in the eponymously named Shanghai Tang shop.) The dining room has traditional lattice-work arches, and doors are effectively lit by Chinese stained-glass inserts.

The 8000 books in the library (on China and western classical music) seem to have been placed there more for decorative reasons than anything else. The battered brown-leather sofa (not actually Winston Churchill's, as a widely spread rumour claims) was salvaged from another club. Private rooms on the third floor are equipped with Czech & Speake showers, video/TV/karaoke machines, and decidedly dubious sofabeds!

It must be said that the overall effect of the place is good; however, there is something unsettling about it, a certain flippant contrivance which leaves a bad saccharine aftertaste. JC

ADDRESS Bank Street
CLIENT David Tang
MTR CENTRAL
ACCESS private

Central

Leese, Robertson & Freeman 1991

Leese, Robertson & Freeman 1991

Hong Kong Club

Situated in the heart of Central, the old four-storey Hong Kong Club had been eyed salaciously by developers for some time. The present building is the result of a deal in which a new club was offered in return for the rights to the irresistible 17-storey void above. This is a good illustration of the attitude to empty space in Hong Kong – it is not considered to have any inherent value in the urban fabric until it is developed.

The colonising of this particular space, however, has led to some ingenious design. The way in which the stack of lettable offices straddles the independent structure of the club is a pure delight, and it is this idea which generates the graceful structure of the whole building. Seidler was one of the seven architects invited to design the Hongkong and Shanghai Bank in 1979 and it was a lucky coincidence that the bank director in charge of the new building was also president of the Hong Kong Club. He commissioned Seidler directly for this project.

The club occupies the four-storey podium and has a private entry in the old axial location facing the square, while the offices are entered from a wide side street. The four massive corner columns (shaped to act as lateral wind braces) are joined by extremely long façade spans, leaving both the club and the offices relatively column-free. The exquisite elegance of these horizontal beams belies the aptness of their geometry. The changing section of the 35-metre concrete beams starts out at both ends as a vertical rectangle (which best resists shear) and smoothly morphs into a deep T-shape (ideal for resisting centre-span bending). These concrete components were made on site from a steel mould which was hoisted up one floor at a time. This method was feasible only because of Hong Kong's low labour costs – elsewhere the beams would have been precast and lifted into place.

The curved walls of the club podium are clad in vertical panels of fawn-

Harry Seidler Associates 1984

Harry Seidler Associates 1984

grey Brazilian granite with a flamed finish. The rest of the exterior is faced in exfoliated Sardinian granite. Typhoon-resisting glass walls screen out excessive sunlight and are framed in dark anodised aluminium. To the south, additional external sunblades are hung from the edges of the floor T-beams. The west façade of the club also used to fulfil a ceremonial role as it was from the third-floor balcony that the Colonial Governor gave his annual salute.

The different levels of the club face on to a stunningly sculptural (reminiscent of Moholy-Nagy) open rotunda. This is topped by the high glass walls of a garden lounge area with a 17-metre-long tapestry designed by Helen Frankenthaler. The fluid and curvilinear volumes swirl in and out and around a cylindrical stair and lift core. Three classic stone arches salvaged from the original entrance portico stand in the first-floor main hall. Although the oscillating plans of the club may seem structurally complex, they use a relatively straightforward method – derived from Josef Albers' theories on 'tensional composition' and 'the balance of unequals', whereby a high degree of variety is achieved solely by the re-arrangement of standard components.

The smooth, creamy whiteness of the materials and the liquidity of the curves create an oddly sinful and indulgent impression, until you realise what the building so closely resembles. Stick a Flake in it! JC

ADDRESS 5 Chater Road
STRUCTURAL ENGINEER Miller Milston & Ferris (Sydney) in association with Palmer & Turner
CONTRACTOR Paul Y Ltd HK
MTR Central
ACCESS none

Harry Seidler Associates 1984

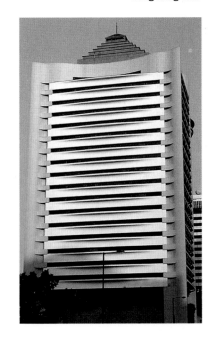

Central

Harry Seidler Associates 1984

Chater Gardens

From 1851 to 1975, Chater Gardens was the site of the Hong Kong Cricket Club, a social and recreational institution of the expatriate community. The Cricket Club still exists but has since been relocated to Wong Nai Chung Gap Road, just above Happy Valley. The garden is named after Sir Paul Chater, a financier (and supposedly keen philanthropist) who was himself an enthusiastic cricketer. Only in Hong Kong do you find statues of and gardens named after financiers rather than the usual war heroes or leaders of state. (A statue of Sir Thomas Jackson of the Hongkong and Shanghai Bank stands in Statue Square to commemorate services rendered to Hong Kong in the financial field.)

Notable for its prime location (admirable for a non-profitable public space), the garden's value per square metre must be one of the highest in the world. A quick roll call of neighbouring buildings gives a good indication of just how high this figure might be: the Ritz Carlton, Hong Kong Hilton, Hong Kong Club, Bank of China, and the Hongkong and Shanghai Bank all occupy sites in the immediate vicinity.

Despite the loud symbolic ringing of cash registers around you, the garden is remarkably peaceful. It is delineated by a covered and lit walkway (supported by marble columns) with profuse vegetation spilling over it (these plants cannot be seen from ground level so must be for the sole benefit of those looking down from the surrounding buildings). Parts of this walkway are hidden by the vegetation and feel very secluded indeed. Because of the height of the trees and shrubs, many of the other paths are partially obscured and provide respite from the hectic surroundings. There is even a large variety of exotic plants to rest your eyes upon. Noise from the nearby traffic is to some extent masked by the pleasing sound of a large two-tiered waterfall. Other water features include a large pond filled with goldfish and water-lilies, contemporary sculpture

Central

Architectural Services Department 1978

Architectural Services Department 1978

(including *Swallows*, 1983, by Chu Hon Sun) and, leading to the water-fall, a row of fountains reminiscent of those at the Tivoli Gardens in Rome. The vegetation is in raised beds and separated from the gently curved paths by diagonal bamboo grids and a low, grey-green and brown stone wall.

On the north side of the garden, two charming little structures (looking peculiarly animal-like with their tall windowed façades facing each other as if huddling together) are clad in grey-green stone. A mosaic staircase rising up between them is surrounded by bamboo and Chinese terracotta pots containing bonsai trees and shrubs. JC

Central

ADDRESS Chater Gardens
MTR Central
ACCESS open

Architectural Services Department 1978

Architectural Services Department 1978

Bank of China

On Garden Road, across from the Hongkong and Shanghai Bank, is the Bank of China's acknowledgement of its financial status in Hong Kong. The 70 storeys of this regional headquarters building – on a steeply sloping 0.8-hectare site in a highly congested part of the Central district – reach 368 metres and dominate the skyline of the island. The building has no definite façade or colour but is a dynamic geometrical gesture that is exciting to look at from all angles. The city itself is reflected in the glazing, which is on a module determined by the grid and expressive structural cross-braces.

Hong Kong lies within a typhoon zone. Tall buildings here have to conform to a wind-load requirement twice that of New York or Chicago, and four times the earthquake equivalent of Los Angeles. Working within these constraints, I M Pei took as his structural metaphor a cane of the bamboo plant – a sturdy, flexible tube with its strength in the outer wall.

The building has no internal structural column. All vertical loads are diverted through the diagonal cross-braces on the outer walls. The building load is then collected and transferred to four massive reinforced-concrete columns, one at each corner of the tower. Compared with a conventional building of similar height, this design reduces the quantity of steel required by almost half.

The asymmetrical form of the tower emerges from a 52-metre-square base. Diagonal lines from each corner divide it into four triangular shafts, each of a different height – defined by a seven-storey diagonal slice – and topped by a glass roof. The north shaft is the first to terminate, followed by the west and east, with the south shaft finally reaching the full height of the tower. The 15-storey-high atrium of the north shaft lends a dramatic impact to the central banking hall, livening up an unexpectedly suppressed and cluttered level.

I M Pei & Partners/Kung & Lee Architects Designers Ltd 1990

I M Pei & Partners/Kung & Lee Architects Designers Ltd 1990

The tower has two entrances, with the main entrance facing south. Due to the geography of the site, these entrances are at different levels and linked by escalators. The lower part of the tower is strangely disappointing. The north entrance features a bizarre double-arched portal and columns covered in charcoal-grey stone tiles. The public banking hall situated on the level above is surrounded by symbolic large green marble columns. The exterior of these two floors is clad with granite, making this whole section look as if it should be somewhere else. The building's structural expression has somehow vanished here; instead, various superficial references attempt to insinuate more meaningful Chinese origins.

Floors 20 to 66 are leased out to tenants; the rest of the building is for the bank's own use. Visit the public viewing gallery on the 47th floor for an excellent overview of the new land reclamation schemes and an unusual view of the Hongkong and Shanghai Bank. AY

ADDRESS 1 Garden Road
CLIENT Bank of China
GROSS FLOOR AREA 135,000 square metres
MTR Central/tram
ACCESS public banking hall and 47th floor open

I M Pei & Partners/Kung & Lee Architects Designers Ltd 1990

Central

I M Pei & Partners/Kung & Lee Architects Designers Ltd 1990

Citibank Plaza

The site for Citibank Plaza, better known by its lot number, 8888, was the last major piece of virgin land in the Central district. The golden opportunity to build here went to a local talent, and the outstanding twin towers now join the list of landmark buildings in the cityscape.

The asymmetrical curved skin is a contextual response to the dominating profile of the nearby Bank of China. Curves and rounded corners emphasise the building's spontaneous form and enable it to project its own identity and character. The two office towers, delightfully curved on some façades, angular on others, rise 40 and 50 storeys to form an L-shape. From the open plaza in front, walkways and footbridges connect various internal nodes and lead to Peak Tram station and Hong Kong Park. While the towers are aligned with the urban axes of the old Central district, the plaza is rotated to respond to the axes of Queensway and the Bank of China, emphasising the continuity of open space between the towers, Chater Gardens and Chater Road.

The language of the building is consistent throughout. The natural finish of the anodised aluminium cladding and flamed granite successfully echoes the coolness of the silver-grey mirrored glass, though an excess of chrome in the entrance lobby creates an unfortunate showy feel. Some of the detailing is ineffectual, but the overall effect of dynamic movement is convincing. However, compared with its neighbours, Citibank Plaza has far less presence. It is trying too hard to cope with its surroundings. AY

ADDRESS 3 Garden Road
SIZE 53,830 square metres
COST HK$1.8 billion
MTR Central
ACCESS open

Rocco Design Partnership 1992

Central

Rocco Design Partnership 1992

Hong Kong Park

In the heart of the busy Central district and surrounded by skyscrapers, more than 10 hectares of densely wooded land with mature trees have been developed, over a period of seven years, into a massive urban park. The intention was to provide pleasant public spaces and sporting facilities for the occupants of the city's overcrowded homes and congested workplaces.

From the central atrium of Pacific Place, external escalators take you to the east entrance. Like many other parks in Hong Kong, this green oasis offers more than you would normally expect from a park. Facilities are evenly spread over the landscape and linked by generous pedestrian walkways and steps.

The focus of the park is an artificial lake set against a rock garden with a 10-metre-high waterfall. The conveniently located registry office near the south entrance has made the lake a popular setting for engagement and wedding photographs. The choice of background for these photographs can be either positively urban (modern skyscrapers) or fictitiously nostalgic (a Roman amphitheatre).

Buildings within the park range from a utilitarian tropical plant house to a popular postmodern observatory tower, from a high-tech see-through aviary to the nostalgic structures of the Tai Chi Garden. The park also accommodates some real historical buildings, such as Flagstaff House (1846), which has been converted into a Museum of Tea Ware. This delightful colonial-style building, originally the home of the commander-in-chief of the British forces, now houses over 500 pieces of earthenware and porcelain.

The sheer scale of Hong Kong Park makes it one of the greatest public projects in recent years. It also provided an opportunity to establish numerous pedestrian connections between areas that were previously

Wong Tung & Partners Ltd 1991

Central

Wong Tung & Partners Ltd 1991

separated. Unfortunately, due to a lack of coherence in its style and design attitude, the park fails to create a dialogue with its overpowering surroundings. AY

LOCATION main entrance in Supreme Court Road
(near Admiralty MTR)
MTR Admiralty
ACCESS open daily 7.00–23.00

Central

Wong Tung & Partners Ltd 1991

Central

Wong Tung & Partners Ltd 1991

Hong Kong Park aviary

This is the project to win over anyone who may have found the book title *The Art of the Structural Engineer* somewhat incongruous. The Hong Kong Park aviary is a breathtaking example of the elegance and expressive beauty which can be achieved in a structural-engineer-led design. A little of the credit, however, goes to the computer (programmer) responsible for the complex geometrical computer calculations which generated the overall form.

The original brief specified a 3000-square-metre enclosure to house a collection of 150 indigenous (south-east Asian) species of birds. The chosen site, a steep-sided valley, kidney-shaped in plan, sits snugly on the curved lower west side of the park bound by Kennedy Road. It is 62 metres wide at its broadest point, with a drop in level of 12 metres over its 75-metre length. The site's main challenge was not only to follow the landscape's tricky shape and form, but also to keep the variety of mature trees on the site. The design of the enclosure therefore had to be sympathetic to the natural shape formed by the canopy of trees, the tallest of which was approximately 13 metres high. (A scheme by another firm, using a traditional mast and mesh system, was rejected because it would have required the removal of too many trees.)

Another interesting challenge of the project was that although the aviary was conceived as the major attraction of the site, it also needed to be as unassertive and unobtrusive as possible. Imagine a demurely attractive aviary!

In 1988, Ove Arup & Partners (in collaboration with the London Lightweight Structures Group) were appointed as consultant structural and geotechnical engineer, and came up with the present design. Their elegant series of arches spans the valley, creating a silhouette undeniably in keeping with the natural curvilinear forms of the site. Three large arches

Central

Wong Tung & Partners Ltd 1991

Wong Tung & Partners Ltd 1991

are used to form the main structure, while a tiny fourth one gives shape to the entrance. The lack of columns (which would have been quite substantial in size) allows the sense of scale within the valley to remain in keeping with the trees, which was always an important concern. Originally, a complicated system of pulleys was envisaged for the erection of the aviary, but this idea was soon replaced when the local contractor chose to cover the entire site with a simpler and more efficient system unique to Hong Kong – bamboo scaffolding. One of the main benefits of this technique was that as no planking is used, the valley floor was left free for other work to continue inside.

During construction, the arches arrived in sections and were butt-welded in position. They were then supported by hand-dug caissons bearing on weathered granite. Spherical bearings were used in order to accommodate the rotations which can occur under wind loading. The graceful curves of the arches (grade 50C steel tubes) were formed by heat induction bending. The arches were then stabilised by doubly curved cable nets which were prestressed and tensioned by rigging screws swaged to the ends and then anchored. The cable nets were built up from stainless-steel cables running in two directions, forming equal-length quadrilaterals, each of which is uniquely skewed. The resultant grid of tensioned cables is what gives the taut mesh enclosure its distinctive undulating form. This mesh envelope is built up from individual strips of woven, crimped stainless-steel wire mesh, which are suspended below the cable nets and arches by a series of hangar bars.

This brilliant nature-inspired design was partly achieved through the use of artificial intelligence. The shape of the supporting arches and the positions and dimensions of the cables were all arrived at by using computer software such as FABLON (a non-linear space-frame analysis

Wong Tung & Partners Ltd 1991

Wong Tung & Partners Ltd 1991

program) and FABCON (a non-linear tension-structure program).

As you walk around the aviary you can see the giant anchorage points of the cables which mark its perimeter. They are bolted to baseplates and cast into concrete piers which project from a continuous boundary wall. The sheer enormity of the components (such as the rigging screws for prestressing the cables) and the various techniques employed are as spectacular as the form of the aviary itself. When looked at up close, the multiple cable anchorage is almost sculptural in its precision. Its beauty lies in the way it tangibly presents the many complex and invisible forces at work within this construction. JC

LOCATION Hong Kong Park
STRUCTURAL ENGINEER Ove Arup & Partners (Lightweight Structures Group)
MTR Admiralty
ACCESS open 9.00–17.00 (admission free)

Wong Tung & Partners Ltd 1991

Central

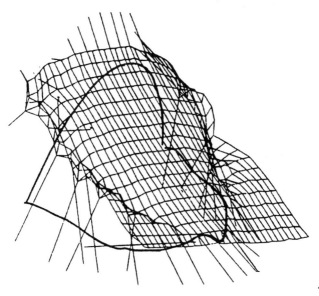

Central

St John's building

This office block stands on one of the most unusual-shaped plots in Hong Kong. Its plan is long, thin and bulbous – a cross between a kidney and a pear. As if that were not awkward enough, this small island plot is completely surrounded by two of the busiest roads in the city, with one, Cotton Tree Drive, rising to a startling height of 12 metres above ground level. Cars whizz by at an alarming and thrillingly close proximity. For office workers inside the building, traffic noise is kept to a minimum by the core wall which acts as a sound barrier.

Situated just north of the western end of Hong Kong Park, the site should have formed a natural junction for parkgoers wishing to extend their walk up towards the Peak. Unfortunately, a slight oversight in pedestrian planning meant that their route would involve throwing themselves into the path of speeding traffic.

The building itself, rectangular in plan, is unusual in that it has no corners – well, no sharp ones, as the four main corners are rounded off. The no-corner theme is followed through at all scales, from the shape of the windows to the directory stand in the lobby. Although this game of curves pleasingly engages the eye, it also appeals to the sense of touch: the walls in the lobby and Peak Tram station area are intriguingly punctured with oval indentations, as if smooth beach pebbles have been pressed into them when soft. The resulting texture is quite sensual, enticing you to run your fingers inside the cool voids.

The reflective finish of the stainless steel ground-floor features, such as the columns and ceiling panels, is continued above in the reflective glass of the windows. The image they give back is usually the greenery of neighbouring trees or the sky, but a most charming thing happens when these windows are viewed from afar. For an instant, those at the four 'corners' (curved in plan) become transparent to reveal the large stainless-steel

KNW Architects + Engineers Ltd 1988

Central

KNW Architects + Engineers Ltd 1988

columns rising up through the interior of the building. This creates a strong impression that the façade is like a taut piece of fabric stretched around the columns and then made rigid, like toffee which has been left to harden. In fact, it is this recurring impression of something that was once fluid that is so appealing. The soft, flowing lines of the building were achieved partly by using a modular cast-aluminium cladding system in preference to sheet aluminium. This ensured a certain flexibility in the casting process of the three-dimensional forms and a higher degree of durability in the larger components.

The most pleasing aspect of the building is its rather retro feel (although unintentional, perhaps). The window shapes are unmistakably evocative of the space capsule aesthetic of the 1950s and '60s. This retro-future atmosphere is, of course, an entirely appropriate intro for the steep climb of the Peak Tram.

The design of the fountain cleverly deals with the changes in level around the building. The fountainhead and surrounding pool are best seen from above, while the cascade is better appreciated from below. From Garden Road there are different views of the cascade's ever-changing display. You can imagine, during particularly heavy monsoon downpours, that the granite steps could themselves become another impromptu cascade. JC

ADDRESS 33 Garden Road
COST HK$71 million
MTR Central
ACCESS open

KNW Architects + Engineers Ltd 1988

Central

KNW Architects + Engineers Ltd 1988

Coda commercial building

This small building is reminiscent of those found sprouting out of the tiniest plots of land in Tokyo. At ten storeys high, it is completely dwarfed by its neighbours here in the heart of Central. The ground-level space is occupied by a pager company. The front and right sides are glazed to reveal a shop filled with electronic gadgetry and components. On the right are computer terminals advertising the company's new Internet services and on the left a large wall of monitors displays stock market information. There is a frenetic buzz as businessmen pop in, push a few buttons, and pop out. The key word here is 'access'. The shop is at most 4 metres wide, with the front façade staggered back. Most of the exterior is silver with chrome details such as the units housing the lighting. Outside, a little row of clear Perspex boxes contains free public phones. On the right side is the main entrance to the rest of the building. A minute lobby clad in black granite contains a (polka-dot!) lift to the other floors. The lobbies above seem even tinier (approximately 1 by 4 metres) but are individually finished to suit the company on that particular floor.

Most floors accommodate a single company (one hairdresser, one beauty salon, one generic faceless office), but on some an unbelievable two companies have been squashed in. The lobbies have dark blue opaque glass panels which cannot be seen through from the outside.

Cute little silver vents stick out of the side of the building. Somehow, there is something about it which makes it appear small and animal-like. JC

ADDRESS 57 Queen's Road
MTR Central
ACCESS open

architect and date unknown

architect and date unknown

Entertainment building

In order to appreciate fully this building you must first see it from the harbour (take a round trip on the Discovery Bay ferry). As you approach Central and your eyes slowly pan across Sheung Wan, the buildings situated immediately on the waterfront can be seen in their entirety, whereas the buildings behind flicker momentarily in and out of view. On a sunny day, when all the glazed façades are shimmering with reflections of the water, the Entertainment building appears like a mirage. The distant image of a tiny castle complete with turrets immediately conjures up Gulliverian images of a magical kingdom. To add to the fantasy, as the top of the building is not easily seen from the street, when you actually arrive to look for the castle you begin to wonder if it was just a figment of your queasy boat-ride imagination.

When you do find the building, although it will not measure up to any fairyland fantasies you may have developed, you won't be disappointed. It is interesting for more down-to-earth reasons. The ground plan, in particular the orientation of the various entrances, is quite unusual. The front façade faces Queen's Road and from this perspective the building seems lopsided, with a curved wing extending out to the left only. The plan is actually very symmetrical, but at a skewed angle to Queen's Road and hence to the other buildings on this road.

The two side streets slope upwards and entrances here bring you in at a higher ground level. Shops at an even lower level have their own separate entrances. The building comprises a one-storey basement, a podium structure and an office tower of 26 floors. The foyer to the latter adjoins a two-storey-high octagonal 'rotunda', which is the focal point of the public concourse. Beige-coloured granite is used on all the façades, with silver-grey glass windows. Topping the building is a pyramid-shaped tin and lead roof.

P & T Architects & Engineers Ltd 1993

P & T Architects & Engineers Ltd 1993

Although its neo-classical style supposedly refers to the Italian Renaissance period, the Entertainment complex is actually more restrained neo-Disney than anything else. This may not sound too promising, but it works. It is interesting and playful yet it satisfies the all-important sense of prestige and formality that Hong Kong businesses look for in an office building. JC

Central

ADDRESS 30 Queen's Road
MTR Central
ACCESS open

P & T Architects & Engineers Ltd 1993

P & T Architects & Engineers Ltd 1993

26 Wellington Street

Fluctuations in the economy affect the streetscape just as much as the changing seasons. If a building does not provide suitable space for its occupants, it will eventually disappear. 26 Wellington Street is an example of a signature building that did not stand the test of time.

Foster Asia had to make sense of a minute footprint at the corner of Wellington Street. Their adaptation of an existing building frame demonstrated that size is not everything in architecture. Within just 55 square metres, the building accommodated a retail unit on the ground and mezzanine floor, five floors of offices, and a plant room on the top floor. With the help of 1-metre-long stainless steel brackets, clear glass panels were fixed onto the existing concrete structure. There was no space for a lift. The access stairs and riser core occupied one third of each floor. This section was expressed on the elevation by a semi-translucent glass-panel system.

The precious full-height curved glass panels on the ground and mezzanine levels have now been taken down and local market traders selling fake brand-name goods and tourist souvenirs have moved in. Toilets have been removed from office floors and two inadequate cubicles installed on the roof. Still, the skin of the building is very much intact. It would be interesting to see what is left of it in a few years' time. AY

ADDRESS 26 Wellington Street
CLIENT The Sun Company Limited
GROSS FLOOR AREA 500 square metres
MTR Central
ACCESS none

Central

Foster Asia (Hong Kong) Ltd 1993

Foster Asia (Hong Kong) Ltd 1993

Lan Kwai Fong Gallery

Lan Kwai Fong is a street packed with bars, restaurants and clubs, crowded with groovy young professionals every night of the week. Facing the street, this first-floor gallery gives the impression that a section of the normal street façade has been stripped away. Its floor-to-ceiling glass panels reveal a bare minimalist interior and glimpses of the exhibits on display. The intervention is simple yet effective.

The gallery supplements the more predictable Lan Kwai Fong activities with an alternative spatial experience. It is as interesting to observe Lan Kwai Fong street life from the gallery as it is to view the gallery from the street. AY

ADDRESS 1F, 5–6 Lan Kwai Fong
MTR Central
ACCESS open

Branko Design Ltd 1995

Central

Branko Design Ltd 1995

Labodega

Vibrant primary colours, flooring of broken tiles, wrought-iron railings, solid masonry walls and twisted columns give Labodega a Latin American atmosphere. Like many bars and small restaurants in the Lan Kwai Fong area, Labodega is spread over several floors. The building is situated at the intersection of Wyndham and D'Aguilar Streets. The former is so steep that the lower floors have direct access to it. Finding your way through the restaurant is an *Alice in Wonderland*-like experience: you go up the stairs from the ground floor only to find yourself still on ground level.

Labodega ('The Barn') serves Spanish and Nuevo Latino food, and its architecture reflects a Spanish influence in a contemporary style. Each floor is treated in a slightly different way to accentuate its function: the dining area on the mezzanine floor incorporates a first-floor balcony, the ground floor serves as the main access floor, and the lower-ground floor with its twisted columns and vaulted ceilings accommodates the wine cellar. AY

ADDRESS 31 Wyndham Street
COST HK$6.5 million
MTR Central
ACCESS open 11.00–15.00, 18.00–24.00

Central

Zanghellini Associates 1993

Zanghellini Associates 1993

Wyndham Street Thai

Another delightful interior by Hernan Zanghellini can be found just across the road from Labodega (see page 128), on the ground floor of a 1960s building. Its minimalist approach brings a new 'up-market' dimension to the local Thai restaurant scene. The whole of the interior, from walls to beams and columns, is covered in rough, grey concrete render. The lighting, arranged to emphasise the full-height, powder-coated fibreglass panels, helps to give the restaurant its unique identity. AY

ADDRESS 38 Wyndham Street
MTR Central
ACCESS open

Central

Zanghellini Associates 1992

Zanghellini Associates 1992

Alleyways

A temporary and vibrant form of architecture found in the alleyways of Central captures the frenetic pace of Hong Kong street life extremely well. In the middle of this ultra-high-gloss financial district, a completely different way of life flourishes in the cracks between the tall buildings. The pedestrian-access-only alleyways between Pedder Street and Pottinger Street (one of the first streets to be paved and laid with steps) which connect Queen's Road to Des Voeux Road are crawling with activity and energy. At Chiu Lung Street, stalls sell refreshments, fruit, umbrellas and knickers. Shoppers also gather round the back of open vans and trucks and yell their bids up to the sellers who hustle their goods with amazing speed. The first piece of architecture here, attached to a fruit stall, is a contraption made of bamboo sticks to display a colourful selection of long umbrellas. It is beautiful and sculptural. In contrast, directly above this, hostile-looking huge steel boxes of services and vents emit a deafening harsh drone.

The architecture of the buildings (whose backs usually face on to the alleyways) is unremarkable at best. Melbourne Plaza, with its main entrance actually opening on to this alleyway, is a prime example. Although quite hideous, it proudly displays its large gaudy black and gold three-triangle insignia. Stairs, which bring the alleyway level with Queen's Road, are followed by a cluster of large picnic umbrella stalls perched over wooden trolley displays on wheels. Variations on these stalls exist all around the city – wherever any small residual spaces are deemed worthy of a little trade activity (which is often).

Douglas Lane has no shops; it is too narrow. There is one stall selling locks, chops and T-shirts, but it is right at the Des Voeux intersection where the alleyway is slightly wider. Elsewhere it is strictly single file. Backing on to this restricted passageway is a restaurant – dark, with some-

thing dripping continuously from some unknown source up above. At first this place seems pretty inhospitable, but when your eyes eventually become adjusted to the lack of light, you can see that someone has lovingly built a pretty, traditional red Chinese archway over the space connecting the sides of the neighbouring buildings.

The next alleyway along, Li Yuen Street East, is a classic. A single row of stalls on the left takes up most of the width. The stalls at the Des Voeux end are completely enclosed by bright green and pink stripey plastic. There are also shops with proper storefronts here. As it is impossible to step back from them to get a front-on view, all signage and displays of goods are peculiarly angled to face the side. Unless you walk sideways, your head cocked at an awkward angle, it is easy to miss the entrance you are looking for.

A typical stall here has a sloped roof sitting on a three-sided structure made of corrugated plastic or steel. This is then framed by steel scaffolding poles which protrude out over the heads of pedestrians and conveniently further extend the space for hanging goods. The poles are then attached to the sides of the buildings at a steep incline by thick cable wire, around which are wrapped strings of lights. Often, instead of these, there is just a bare bulb hanging. Behind each stall are individual locked electrical and services boxes. JC

ADDRESS between Pedder and Pottinger Streets (connecting Des Voeux Road and Queen's Road)
MTR Central
ACCESS open

Central

Bamboo scaffolding

The bamboo scaffolding of Hong Kong follows a traditional Chinese building practice and is used extensively on almost all kinds of construction projects. The main advantage of bamboo poles over steel ones is that they form a lighter, more flexible and cheaper structure. They also cope well with tensile stress, and there is a certain beauty in their extreme low-tech appearance.

Bamboo (which is a type of grass, not a tree) gets its remarkable strength from the hollow cylindrical form of its stem, which comprises a thick rigid outer and inner layer filled with tightly packed fibre. Sections are sealed off (by the horizontal parts produced by its segmented growth pattern) at various intervals, which can be identified by the ringed marks on the outside of the stem. The poles are roughly between 6.7 and 7.6 metres long and are imported from the Guangdong province of China.

On a typical high-rise building project, the bamboo scaffolding will be divided into three parts. The first base tier (where the compression load is greatest) is composed of strong Chinese Fir poles. Next, a type of thick, heavy bamboo pole is set out on a grid approximately 3 metres by 3 metres, and this is followed by a thinner, lighter bamboo grid at a quarter of this size. Finally, huge cross-bracing Chinese Fir poles are used to stabilise the whole structure. Sometimes 'catch fans' (to catch potentially dangerous falling fragments) are cantilevered out at an upward sloping angle. The whole structure is then usually covered in green, gauzy, web-like nylon mesh and the plastic Chinese material that is used to make those stripey bags that one sees everywhere.

Apparently there is a trade rule which states that scaffolding must be dismantled by the person who erected it. The reasons given are a mixture of superstition and practicality, but the rule is probably upheld mainly in order to ensure that scaffold erectors do the complete job.

The scaffolding profession even has its own deity, different from that of the building trade. It does, however, share its deity with Cantonese opera troupes – not entirely coincidental as bamboo is also used for the construction of traditional opera stages.

In 1986, at the international Expo in Vancouver, Hong Kong was represented by a structure entirely enclosed by bamboo scaffolding. JC

Central

LOCATION any building site, anywhere in Hong Kong
FURTHER INFORMATION can be found in *Bamboo Scaffolding in Hong Kong* by Stephen Lau Siu and Lee Ho Yin

Admiralty and Wanchai

Lippo Centre

The Lippo Centre development is very revealing in terms of the complex and idiosyncratic nature of Hong Kong planning laws. This prime site of reclaimed waterfront flatland became available when the air rights over Admiralty station interchange were sold. This procedure was devised by the Hong Kong government (a major MTR shareholder) to help fund the development of the transport system. The image of a vacant plot with a 'for sale' sign is quite alien to modern Hong Kong developers. They are more likely to be squeezing sites out of intangible sources by buying air rights or agreeing to provide public spaces in exchange for air rights.

The project was initially intended to filter some of the corporate and financial institutions away from the Central district. Paul Rudolph had envisioned the Bond Centre (its original name), the Hong Kong Bank headquarters and the planned Bank of China as a triumvirate of 'focal buildings', in line with his theory regarding hierarchical groupings. According to Rudolph, most buildings should be background buildings, with only a few standing out as gateways or landmarks in the cityscape. As a city-planning concept, the project also served as a vehicle to test another of his long-held concerns: the segregation of pedestrian and vehicular traffic into different layers. For this reason some of the most important considerations in the planning of the Lippo Centre were the first-floor linkages into the existing pedestrian network which joins Admiralty to Central and its already extensive footpath system.

The basic design of the centre – two hexagonal towers clad in solar reflective glass on a podium connected to Admiralty's elevated pedestrian network – is quite simple. (Another of Rudolph's obsessions is the problem of scale in skyscrapers; he believes that so long as the first 30 metres or so are of a scale that people can respond to, the tower above can be scaleless.) The towers are divided into three vertical segments in

Paul Rudolph 1988

Admiralty and Wanchai

Paul Rudolph 1988

an effort to break the massive scale into comprehensible parts. This, however, immediately gives the building an anthropomorphic reading with distinct robotic/humanoid dimensions (head, torso, legs), a seemingly obvious paradox in a discussion of scale. A single, more intricately faceted storey at the top and bottom of each division is cantilevered to reveal floor soffits, roofs, and two sides on the exterior. The intention behind this is based on the assumption that a single floor can be easily recognised by most people, and that it would help impart a human scale to the multi-storey building.

Grey plastic-looking Lego legs (try not to visualise a giant Lego hole in the soffit for the leg to fit into) ranging in height from three to eight storeys are meant to be read as 'hydraulic pumps propelling the building into the sky' – a dangerous reading as, with this in mind, the view below seems even more unstable.

Inside, the building's main lobby of tasteful cream and a muted but glossy granite finish is somehow disappointing, especially if you were hoping for something akin to the inside of a giant robot. The multi-layer base was conceived as 'pools' of spaces which would cascade, flow and swirl around the great columns. This analogy to the circulation of water could prove problematic as not everyone wants to cascade into a space. In comparison, the corridors of the floors above seem extremely pokey. Spaces are narrow, almost cramped, with very little natural daylight. In fact, in terms of scale, the transition from the opulent lobby below to these tight and stingy spaces only accentuates the sense of confusion.

Twelve basic plans are used for the towers, with each floor rotated at an angle of 45 degrees over the floor below. In total – over its three different vertical transportation zones and the additional two refuge floors in each tower – there is a total of 58 different plans within the 76

Paul Rudolph 1988

Paul Rudolph 1988

office floors. Conceptually, the cantilevered floor sections are supposed to work like the branches of a tree, each growing out to obtain its own share of space, air and sun. In less poetic terms, these octagonal leaves (four narrow and four wide) conveniently supply view-obsessed executives with highly coveted corner offices.

Nicknames or local interpretations (including koala bear, robot, bamboo stalk, Chinese frieze patterns) suggest that attempts to make the building's scale more readable have not been successful. Still, the architecturally derided habit of viewing buildings as objects is not without merit for it often endears a building to the public, and in Hong Kong, how a building appears from Victoria Peak is important. Hong Kong Tai Tai often appreciate the gem-like qualities of a building, and their obsession with a stone's ability to *seem gong* (reflect light) is not entirely inappropriate. The shimmery surfaces reflecting the harbour make the towers look like a stack of melting ice cubes – if you look carefully you might even see a subliminal message (is that an 's'?). Given the vast diversity of interpretations, the Lippo Centre is a sort of architectural Rorschach test – you see what you want to see. Go to the roof of the neighbouring mall, lie down, look up and daydream – it'll be cheaper than your shrink.
JC

ADDRESS 89 Queensway
CLIENT Bond Corporation International Ltd (original building), Admiralty Development Ltd (Lippo Centre)
STRUCTURAL ENGINEER Wong & Ouyang (Hong Kong) Ltd
CONTRACTOR Hip Hing Construction Co. Ltd
MTR Admiralty
ACCESS public areas open

Paul Rudolph 1988

Paul Rudolph 1988

Far East Finance Centre

This office block is entirely clad in solar-reflective gold-tinged glass. It is basically a giant gold ingot standing on end – the quintessential Hong Kong building. JC

ADDRESS 16 Harcourt Road
MTR Admiralty
ACCESS lobby only

Wong & Ouyang 1982

Wong & Ouyang 1982

Cappucci

In what can only be interpreted as a friendly gesture, the little alien space-craft sitting in the corner of one of the pedestrian walkways of Admiralty has been seen to dispense frothy cups of cappuccino and ciabatta sandwiches to all who approach. This silver, saucer-shaped coffee/snack bar has a roller shutter which slides back to reveal a waist-high opening angled towards the pedestrian flow passing in and out of the Supreme Court and Queensway Government Offices.

The interior has steel storage units and a floorspace which just about accommodates the three amiable staff found within its confines. A hidden side door reveals an inventive hydraulic system which lowers the platform floor to ground level, making it easier to exit and enter and allowing for wheelchair access.

This is believed to be a first encounter of its kind and, apparently, if no adverse conditions are found and allies are forthcoming, more will descend elsewhere in Hong Kong. JC

Admiralty and Wanchai

LOCATION just outside the Supreme Court, on a raised platform walkway running parallel to Queensway
MTR Admiralty
ACCESS open

architect and date unknown

architect and date unknown

Pacific Place

As British armed forces began to depart in the early 1980s, giant plots of land appeared in their wake. One of these, the former Victoria Barracks, was snapped up by Swire Properties for its massive commercial development of four separate lots: two taken up by Pacific Place, and one each for the Hong Kong Park and a new Supreme Court/office block. The most interesting aspect of the project – besides its sheer size – is the steep slope of the site, which has a 26-metre difference between some of the levels. (There is also the interesting Japanese soldier ghosts problem to consider.)

The project had two phases. When the developers were given the go-ahead for phase 1, in true no-time-to-lose Hong Kong style, a flexible design was soon produced in which the uncertainty of phase 2 was simply one of the criteria. The synchronisation of the two phases became crucial as construction had to begin even before the whole site had been bought. The completed project includes two rectangular towers (one of 36 storeys for office use and a 40-storey Marriott hotel with 609 rooms and 140 atrium apartments); two elliptical towers (a 36-storey Conrad hotel with 511 rooms and 240 parkside apartments, and the 50-storey Shangri-la Hotel with 566 rooms and 65,000 square metres of office space); a mall on four floors (a 65,000-square-metre temple for the beloved god of consumerism); a cinema complex and a parking lot for 650 cars. To simplify both design and construction you might have thought that the best approach would be to abandon any attempt at unity and try to tackle the project in bite-sized pieces. In fact it was thought that the visual aspect of the design simply did not need to adhere to the different structural designs and construction methods used. One elliptical tower used radial beams projecting out from a central corewell to the perimeter steel columns, whereas the other used a flat-slab construction supported by

Admiralty and Wanchai

Wong & Ouyang (Hong Kong) Ltd 1988 and 1991

steel wing panels and factory-made steel columns. But they still ended up looking the same – mainly because of the grey reflective glass window walls and white metal horizontal cladding pieces used on both structures.

However, other examples of this matter-of-fact approach have produced some gems. In their rectangular building, architects Wong & Ouyang increased the number of double-aspect corner offices (much favoured by senior Hong Kong executives) by slicing off the corners to create … hey presto … more corners! Here a certain idiocy has given rise to cleverness and ingenuity.

Somehow Pacific Place does not overwhelm. The many changes in level conveniently distinguish the various parts and serve as a natural key to the understanding of the project as a whole. The interior finish has been left clean and simple in white and stainless steel with pale grey terrazzo floors. Compared with most Hong Kong malls, there is a noticeable lack of ornamentation (to allow for the special festive decor which marks each new season). However, this does not explain the cheap-lounge look of the see-through diamond-shaped Perspex prisms above the main foyer area.

Still, the place works. Feel the ease. Step out of the MTR and let the cool 7.5-metre-wide bridge gently guide you (you will offer little or no resistance) towards the charms of the effortless Pacific Place. JC

ADDRESS Pacific Place, Queensway
GROSS FLOOR AREA 490,000 square metres
COST HK$1.3 billion (phase 1); HK$3.2 billion (phase 2)
MTR Admiralty
ACCESS open

Wong & Ouyang (Hong Kong) Ltd 1988 and 1991

Wong & Ouyang (Hong Kong) Ltd 1988 and 1991

Zen

After having successfully opened Zens in London and Montreal, restaurateur (and Cantonese video importer) Leung opened this Hong Kong branch in 1988. The difference here is that this 500-seater restaurant is serving Chinese food to a Chinese city. Not exactly a novelty in itself until you consider the appearance of the restaurant. It is decidedly un-Chinese – an interesting if dubious choice.

According to a review in a French interior design magazine, Zen represents an oasis of good design in a metropolis which has yet to discover a good design sense. The review also notes that Zen is peerless in its understated minimalism. Interestingly, however, in the nine years since its opening there has been no outbreak of copycat designs. The reason why this particular import has not caught on is probably that in a city with a healthy lust for the ornate, Zen seems to take itself too seriously. Zero marks for context here as someone seems to have failed to understand the local temperament. A lack of decoration is seen as morbid: basically, minimalism equals death. Whatever were they thinking?

Still, certain parts do work. The curvy glass façade lets diners look out on to one of the open spaces of the mall, usually filled with a temporary exhibition. It is a shame that the tables aren't actually placed against this wall, fitting snugly into its curves. The view from the outside is obscured by opaque glass, but wouldn't vapour from the nearby stack of bamboo steamers provide a more natural and appealing screen – and be more effective in drawing in a hungry passer-by? More opaque glass separates private dining areas from the main space. This is redundant most of the time as it fragments the space and makes it difficult to achieve the Chinese concept of *go hing* (noisy, joyful and vibrant) so necessary in a dim sum hall. Intimate dining is an alien concept – and never a prerequisite for good dim sum.

Rick Mather 1988

Rick Mather 1988

The focus of the restaurant is a 21-metre-long serpentine structure made from a series of 26 glass bowls suspended from a track on the ceiling. The bowls sit in brushed stainless-steel cradles which hang off stainless-steel cables tensioned between the ceiling and floor duct. Water is pumped up to the top bowl via a flexible hose (which looks like an adapted hand-held shower attachment). The water then travels down through each bowl via a precisely placed outlet. Disney stuff really – a new interpretation of the naughty flamboyance implied by overflowing champagne glasses – but very Hong Kong. It is precisely this feeling of excess that gets the adrenaline flowing here. Somehow, though, the showiness and minimalism strike a discordant note. You can't help thinking that they could have gone even further and had a few koi swimming around, or at least coloured water. There is no point in being tasteful about this sort of thing.

There is also a mysterious aspect to this interior. As your eyes follow the water display up towards the ceiling, looking for its source, you are greeted with bare concrete and an extremely rough-looking finish, complete with exposed service ducts. How does this fit in with the clean simple lines of modernity below? Did they run out of money or is this an obscure design detail? Is it a delineation of space, a sort of dining-room-meets-ceiling-interface architectonic thing? Why is this area exposed and the floor duct encased in marble? Suddenly the minimalism just seems tired and restrained. Which leads to the question, 'Is there something inherently frustrating about opaque glass?' JC

ADDRESS Pacific Place, Queensway
CLIENT Lawrence Leung
MTR Admiralty
ACCESS open

Rick Mather 1988

Rick Mather 1988

British Consulate

'The building was to be fine in appearance, welcoming, definably British and geared to projecting British interests.' The FCO brief for this project sounds as if it was written by someone trying to stifle the overwhelming sense of emotion which has characterised this project from the start.

Because the structures are spread around the site perimeter in plan, there is a definite air of defiance about the front elevation. In fact, the complex as a whole has the stout posture of a bulldog. Apparently 'Britishness' was designed into the elevations, which are meant to look 'well groomed, well tailored and disciplined in composition'. There seems to be a slight confusion here as surely the brief was looking for a building which would symbolise the continuing interest of the British government in Hong Kong, not a suit. JC

Admiralty and Wanchai

ADDRESS 1 Supreme Court Road, Admiralty
CLIENT HM Government, Overseas Estates Department
STRUCTURAL ENGINEER Ove Arup & Partners, HK
CONTRACTOR Laing-Hip Hing joint venture
MTR Admiralty
ACCESS to public areas

Terry Farrell & Partners 1997

Terry Farrell & Partners 1997

Central Plaza

I M Pei's architectural masterpiece, the Bank of China, has dominated the skyline of Hong Kong for some time, but now a less dignified triangular structure, covered with gold and silver, has sprung up and grabbed all the attention. At 373.9 metres, Central Plaza is the tallest reinforced-concrete building in the world.

This 78-storey office tower, with its pyramid hat touching 310 metres at its apex, dominates the Wanchai seafront. But the format of this megastructure is disappointingly familiar. Beneath the tower is a 30-metre-high podium block surmounted by offices. A sky lobby on the forty-sixth floor is open to the public and affords a great view of the city. The triangular configuration with its recessed edges provides six corner offices per floor (and corner offices are worth more). This clever arrangement allows two thirds of the façade offices to have a view of the sea.

The self-important podium serves as a grand entrance lobby and features a huge kitsch motif in green marble which is repeated *ad nauseam* throughout the building. At the entrance, these unbearable features, accompanied by four 6-metre-high palm trees and scaled-down versions of the entrance columns by the escalators, welcome visitors to 'the tallest building in Asia'. But after a while, the effect becomes quite amusing and an enjoyable contrast to the dull MTR station. At night the building is radiant in gold neon and floodlighting, while the glass pyramid (Top of the Town) glows in a range of ever-changing colours. AY

ADDRESS 18 Harbour Road, Wanchai
SITE AREA 230 square metres SIZE 30,140 square metres
COST HK$1250 million
MTR Wanchai
ACCESS public areas open

Dennis Lau & Ng Chen Man 1992

Dennis Lau & Ng Chen Man 1992

The Academy for Performing Arts

Just off the buzzing Wanchai district, an evocative and refined structure sits calmly by Victoria Harbour. Financed by the Royal Hong Kong Jockey Club, the building was designed to be an easily identifiable landmark. Before its construction, the site was divided into a number of triangular sections by existing services – an underground railway line, water supply pipes and sewage reserves – but rather than seeing this as a constraint, the architect has taken advantage of these separate areas to create a dramatic complex.

Covered entirely with large, heavily textured stone tiles, the structure is interesting to look at from all angles. Public activity areas – an interior central atrium and an outdoor performance platform – are clearly defined by overhanging space-frames. Gentle curves were introduced to the exterior landscape in order to soften the angular shape of the building.

From the moment you enter the academy, you are transported into a silent, monotone environment designed for the creation of harmonious melody and intricate movements. Daylight filters through a fully glazed triangular space-frame into the generous central atrium. Different activities radiating from this space make it a focal point of the building and a popular meeting place for students of the various schools.

The complex includes schools for drama, music, dancing and theatre technology. Its vehicular entrance is achieved by introducing an internal road which separates the building into two blocks at ground level. The Academy block houses practice rooms and studios, while the Theatre block accommodates recording halls and TV studios in addition to a 1200-seat rectangular theatre. Above ground level, the two blocks are connected. The interior of the building is less angular than it appears from the outside. Large volumes have been reserved for theatres, back stage space and studios.

Simon Kwan & Associates Ltd 1985

Simon Kwan & Associates Ltd 1985

Acoustic engineering was a particularly important consideration with this building. In places where a high degree of sound insulation is required, the inner wall floats on resilient pads to isolate acoustic vibration and prevent it travelling through the structure. AY

ADDRESS 1 Gloucester Road, Wanchai
CLIENT The Royal Hong Kong Jockey Club
COST HK$300 million
MTR Wanchai
ACCESS certain areas open

Simon Kwan & Associates Ltd 1985

Simon Kwan & Associates Ltd 1985

Hong Kong Arts Centre

The original 1969 plan was to house the Hong Kong Arts Centre in either a floor of an existing building or a renovated cinema. The thought of a purpose-built centre did not occur until eight years later (this shocking lack of urgency, by Hong Kong standards, applies only to non-profitable projects) when the Hong Kong government eventually granted the scheme a small piece of free land. This freebie, however, did not extend to any funds for the construction: this relied entirely on donations. The project only became feasible when a deal was struck in which the top seven floors of offices would pay for the arts accommodation below. At this point the brief rapidly grew and the requirements imposed on the centre snowballed out of proportion as the visual, musical, dramatic and performing arts all vied for space on the tiny 30-metre by 30-metre site. The final shopping list included a 200-seat recital hall, a 100-seat studio theatre, a rehearsal room, a 463-seat theatre, an exhibition gallery with sculpture terrace, restaurants, a members' club, artists' studios, musical practice rooms and, of course, a considerable amount of rentable office space (for cultural organisations).

Tightness of space was not the only physical constraint. The building sits on the Wanchai reclamation site, where the soil is very soft and the water table is only 2 metres below ground. The reinforced-concrete building was therefore constructed on top of a 2-metre-thick concrete raft. Below this, at an average depth of 33 metres, there are 303 piles (with a diameter of 55 centimetres) supporting the building.

The difficulties do not end here. Because the corner site is sandwiched between two large buildings, neither windows nor access was possible on those two sides. This constraint is skilfully resolved in the design of the plan. An L-shaped service core runs along the side of the two neighbouring buildings to house the staircases, lifts, lavatories, mechanical

Tao Ho Design Architects 1977

Tao Ho Design Architects 1977

equipment and storerooms. The space thus created contains the various functions of the centre in an unconventional stacked layout, and it is in this feature that the ingenuity of the building lies. Against all odds, a decent-sized gallery has been achieved, as well as an innovative vertical (and asymmetrical) foyer.

The other components also manage to carve out their own space, occasionally breaking out horizontally to create a satisfying expression of their function on the outside of the building. For example, the heavy solid forms of the auditorium and galleries which jut out over the entrance can be easily distinguished from the open glazed façade of the restaurant and the repeated motifs of the eight floors of offices above.

There is no danger, however, of having too many disparate elements. Although different materials are used, everything has roughly the same metallic grey finish. Everything, that is, save the service ducts, expressed by two red vertical strips which run up the full height of the building (joined by a post-tensioned perimeter beam at the eighth floor) and unify the contrasting elements which they frame. There is also a good sense of unity between the structural and the decorative design since the same triangular motif is used throughout. By using a basic design unit and repeating it in the floor plan, on the ceiling structural grid and on the external spandrels (trusses of fibreglass triangular formwork), the architects were employing a technique with strong historical precedence, for this is the traditional Chinese method of expressing structure.

In the central five-storey void hangs a delightful bright yellow sculpture. But the artwork in question is not an exhibit but a massive air-conditioning duct, reminding us that this building does not take itself too seriously. Like a breath of fresh air, it stands out against the sad granite aesthetic of its corporate neighbours. Unlike most buildings in this city,

Tao Ho Design Architects 1977

Tao Ho Design Architects 1977

the centre is not trying to look expensive, and this lack of pretension strikes you as somehow being honest and has you rooting for its success.

After 20 years, an unavoidable shabbiness has set in, making it an increasingly endearing little underdog of a building. In a subtle way, it is as close as you get to an alternative space in Hong Kong. JC

ADDRESS 2 Harbour Road, Wanchai
CLIENT Hong Kong Arts Centre
COST HK$5 million
MTR Wanchai
ACCESS open

Tao Ho Design Architects 1977

Tao Ho Design Architects 1977

Albron Court

This unusual 29-storey residential tower is an expression of the city's intricate living environment. A typical residential floor comprises four living units, with the central lift core and stairs dividing these units into two sections. Partition walls between the units on each side allow for flexibility when different combinations of apartments are required.

This complexity is expressed through the tower's articulate floor plans. All units are orientated so as to take full advantage of the views of either the mountains or Victoria Harbour from their balconies.

The domestic tower has a structural wall system, while the commercial floors and car park below are supported by a column-and-grid system. Apartments on the 20th floor and above are colour coded and set back, allowing their roofs to be used as open-air roof gardens and private swimming pools. The red central core houses the exposed escape stairs which continue up to the highest point of the building.

The boldness and expression of this tower have made it a focal point for the area. AY

ADDRESS 99 Caine Road, Admiralty
COST HK$48 million
MTR Sheung Wan
ACCESS none

Ronald Poon Associates 1985

Ronald Poon Associates 1985

Causeway Bay

Golden Lee Theatre

This cinema is housed inside the new Lee Theatre Plaza – a development named after and built on the site of an old landmark, the French-styled art deco Lee Theatre. The funny little domed skylight perched on the low front section of the building is supposed to be a reproduction of a feature from the original building. Someone must have really taken a shine to this unremarkable feature (in reproduction anyway) as it is repeated 122 metres further up on the twenty-second floor, above the stack of three-storey-high atrium spaces. This strange habit of reproducing bits of an old building is quite popular in Hong Kong and is probably an outcome of the guilt felt after the destruction of something nostalgic. For the most part these reproductions are unsatisfying and quite arbitrary.

The first of the curved glass atrium spaces is double height and just about low enough to be visible from street level. And it is this relationship between the cinema lobby and the traffic intersection below which has been played upon by the architects. The use of a ceiling sign (tilted for an optimum view from the intersection) to light the space deviates from the migraine-inducing glare (typical of this area) of the spaces above. However, since the lighting is relatively subdued, the sign, although distinct, fails miserably in its efforts to be noticed. Still, it does keep the glare off the video wall.

The first lobby is actually on a lower level and contains Perspex walls patterned with overlapping layers of green adhesive panetone. Both bright and translucent, they suggest the playfulness of a layered jelly. The idea for the mural behind the ticket booth was borrowed from earlier Hong Kong cinemas where hand-painted marquees – usually depicting close-ups of featured stars – were used extensively. A closed-circuit camera takes random images of waiting customers and projects them on to the video wall in the upper lobby. Technically, you should be able to

Wong & Choy Architecture 1995

Wong & Choy Architecture 1995

see your friends in the lobby as you approach the cinema. However, like the single bullet theory, it works beautifully on paper but in reality remains a ludicrous impossibility.

Other features of the cinema include a captivating large blue dome in one of the upper lobby's alcoves. The void is flooded in blue light thereby blurring the distinction between the concave surface of the dome and the light itself. This not only gives it a two-dimensional quality, but makes the light seem like a solid component – not an entirely inappropriate theme to explore in a cinema.

Inside the viewing rooms, perforated metal panels react to changes in light immediately before and after a film, and the walls of diagonally cut panels temporarily reveal the mechanism behind and draw attention to the gadgetry necessary for the projection of the illusory world on the screen. JC

ADDRESS Lee Theatre Plaza, 99 Percival Street
CLIENT Lee Theatre Realty
CONTRACTOR E-Pont Interiors Ltd
MTR Causeway Bay, exit towards Lee Theatre Plaza or Times Square
ACCESS open

Wong & Choy Architecture 1995

Causeway Bay

Wong & Choy Architecture 1995

New York Cinema

The ground-floor entrance and ticket booth have a traditional movie-house layout where an island booth with windows on opposite sides is centred in the space (ticket sellers sit back to back) so that two queues can be dealt with at the same time. A dramatic black-and-white marble checkerboard floor helps to draw passers-by into the lobby, which is hung with posters advertising current films.

The ticket booth is made of shiny copper plates riveted together. It looks rather odd – a sort of disco-ed ship hull – for the industrial aesthetic of the rivets is somehow incongruous with the dazzlingly shiny copper. This material extends to the ceiling where it forms a radiating pattern, and from these extensions hang little film posters in case you forget which film you've come to see.

The next space you pass through, the hallway/lift lobby, is the most interesting part of the cinema. A rectangular hole has been cut into the edge where the wall meets the ceiling. No doubt influenced by the artist James Turrell's use of light to create illusions of space, these holes (which house the lighting) use the whiteness of the hollows to radiate light from a hidden source. The edges of the holes are angled to a sharp corner to conceal their thickness, giving an interesting two-dimensional effect. There is a slight indentation in the wall just below hip height, supposedly so that you can lean your foot against it while waiting for the lift. Although it looks as if it might have been an afterthought, how thoughtful if it wasn't!

A staircase leading to the top floor has a steel balustrade (custom made in Los Angeles) whose railing extends to form a display case which, unfortunately, looks unused. A space-frame ceiling houses the sprinkler system. The amount of artificial light in the Causeway Bay area means that the windows can be used as a light source in the evening as well as the daytime.

Wong & Ouyang (Hong Kong) Ltd 1992

Wong & Ouyang (Hong Kong) Ltd 1992

This could be seen as a form of energy efficiency if it didn't highlight the gross energy consumption of the area in general. Toilets have hand-sanded Plexiglass ceilings which look like ice cubes – and which probably have a favourable effect on cold drink sales. JC

Causeway Bay

ADDRESS 463–483 Lockhart Road
MTR Causeway Bay
ACCESS open

Wong & Ouyang (Hong Kong) Ltd 1992

Wong & Ouyang (Hong Kong) Ltd 1992

Hong Kong stadium

The stadium is a piece of precise structural geometry in a random geological setting. The challenge of the brief was to provide a structure capable of hosting international sporting and entertainment events for 40,000 people while taking up no more of the site than the previous stadium which accommodated only 28,000.

Seating is divided into three decks, with the top level cantilevered over the surrounding ring road and projecting out towards the heavily vegetated hillsides. The utility level – containing changing rooms, food services and plant and administration rooms – is under the main concourse, below ground level in some areas. Public entry is on the west side, where all spectators are invited into the stadium by the grand structural gesture of the roof arches which ascend from the landscaped staircase and extend along the entire street frontage. From the best seats in the stadium (centre-top of the east-side bowl) the entire seating arrangement, roof structure, pitch and surrounding So Kun Po valley can all be appreciated.

The Teflon-coated fibreglass roof on a lightweight steel frame covers 75 per cent of the seating and spans 240 metres across the stadium. At night the roof fabric is illuminated in a dramatic celebration of the structure's heroic outline. A high degree of finish and a consistency in the use of materials and design details contribute to the stadium's fine aesthestic.

Special attention has been paid to spectator safety. Ramps, staircases and numerous exits provide a carefully distributed system that allows up to 50,000 people to be evacuated within 11 minutes. AY

ADDRESS 1 Stadium Path, So Kun Po
MTR Causeway Bay
ACCESS limited

Causeway Bay

Hellmuth, Obata & Kassabaum 1994

Causeway Bay

Hellmuth, Obata & Kassabaum 1994

Public toilets, Victoria Park

The Hing Fat Street public toilets were the result of an exceptional architectural competition (a rare occurrence in Hong Kong) and cost a staggering HK$13 million to construct. This urban folly fulfils two basic functions: it is both a public toilet serving the street and Victoria Park, and a clever iconic entrance to the park from Hing Fat Street. A small courtyard space (providing alternative access to the park) gives a breathing space between the busy street and the toilet facilities. A guard house and barrier are located at the park entrance to control opening hours and regulate vehicular access.

Given its location – close to tennis courts, basketball pitches and a busy street – the actual enclosure is surprisingly small, and there are no changing rooms or facilities to support these activities. The use of high-level openings (for natural ventilation) and translucent materials makes the building exceptionally bright and airy. Glimpses of the park beyond provide a sense of orientation and relate the structure to its surroundings.

Although this piece of architecture has undoubtedly improved the environment, it is in fact a simple building and no different from other public toilets in the city. The use of many different colours and materials is confusing. Also, a lack of consistency in the composition invites many unnecessary bits and pieces and makes the project seem more complicated than it really is. As a prototype for the city, the structure lacks a clear identity, despite its exorbitant cost. AY

Causeway Bay

LOCATION Hing Fat Street
COST HK$13 million
MTR Tin Hau
ACCESS open

Lo King Leung, Chang Ping Hung, Lo Chi Sing 1994

Lo King Leung, Chang Ping Hung, Lo Chi Sing 1994

Oscar's

Situated on the third floor of the shopping arcade of the World Trade Centre, Oscar's – depending on the time of day – is a café/bar/restaurant. The architect has taken two private units of a normal shopping mall and transformed them into a welcoming public space.

The project sits conveniently in front of the escalator which brings potential customers up from the second floor. The first branch of Oscar's in Lan Kwai Fong is a regular meeting place for trendy young expats. Oscar's at the World Trade Centre attracts a more mixed clientele into its wide-open see-through interior, which is simple, uncluttered and predominantly white. The café, bar and restaurant areas are designed to be operated as individual units. By employing hidden roller shutters (which close down one department without affecting the other two), the manager has total control over how much space is in use at any time.

Oscar's works predominantly as a sandwich and coffee bar during the day and a restaurant/wine bar at night. There are three main areas: the café which opens internally to the shopping mall, the restaurant with its view out to Victoria Harbour, and the bar in between. The areas are cleverly separated so that you don't actually notice the restaurant from the entrance unless you are consciously looking for it. The bar makes a subtle yet effective partition between the 130-seat restaurant and the sandwich-serving café. JC

ADDRESS 3rd floor, World Trade Centre
COST HK$5 million
SIZE 320 square metres
MRT Causeway Bay
ACCESS open 9.00–24.00

Causeway Bay

Tonkins Design Limited 1996

Tonkins Design Limited 1996

Tsim Sha Tsui

Hong Kong Cultural Centre

Although originally there were misgivings about the project, over the years the Hong Kong public seems to have established a stable, almost loving relationship with its cultural centre. The main disappointment arose out of the justifiably high expectations which existed for the site. The land was formerly occupied by the Kowloon–Canton Railway terminus (whose 80-year-old clock tower you can still see), and it was hoped that its place would be taken by a momentous design which could represent Hong Kong and its culture and be seen by the international ships passing through the harbour – and possibly feature on the face of the millions of postcards sent from the city each year. The site now comprises the Hong Kong Space Museum with its auditoriums and ancillary buildings, the Hong Kong Museum of Art, the Salisbury Garden and the Tsim Sha Tsui public pier.

The pink ceramic wall tiles used extensively on the exterior of the buildings led to one of the most popular (and hurtfully unforgettable) accusations – that it looked like a large toilet. However, this feeling seems to have passed, due to the barrage of events (a total of 836 functions last year) which assails the centre, drumming home the idea that in terms of function it is successful.

The main structure with its exaggerated pitched roof and splayed base (covered walkways) contains a 2085-seat concert hall, a 1734-seat grand theatre, the main foyer, rehearsal and practice rooms, an exhibition gallery, an art library and restaurants, and attracts 800,000 people a year. The Museum of Art has six exhibition galleries, a variety of support and educational facilities (including conservation laboratories and storage), a 150-seat lecture hall, visual art studios, and group reception rooms.

On any given day the steps outside the main foyer are occupied by one or more wedding parties having their picture taken. This could be

Tsim Sha Tsui

Architectural Services Department 1980, 1989, 1991

Tsim Sha Tsui

Architectural Services Department 1980, 1989, 1991

construed as praise of sorts for the buildings, but in fact the real backdrop of desire is across the harbour – the collective buildings of Central.

The best time of the year to see the cultural centre is New Year's Eve, when everyone gathers by the waterfront, fully equipped with camera and tripod, to capture the festive illuminations on the buildings for the first pages of their photo album. Despite the fact that the centre itself is not a particularly brilliant subject for a photo opportunity, it has certainly found a role as a great vantage point and venue – which perhaps was its true and humble intention. JC

Tsim Sha Tsui

ADDRESS 10 Salisbury Road
CLIENT Hong Kong Government
and Urban Council
MTR Tsim Sha Tsui
ACCESS open

Architectural Services Department 1980, 1989, 1991

Tsim Sha Tsui

Architectural Services Department 1980, 1989, 1991

Felix restaurant

The journey through this series of spaces designed by Philippe Starck begins with an elevator ride to the top floor of the newly built 30-floor extension to the historic Peninsula Hotel. As you reach the final floor, there is a great sense of drama as the lift lights dim and other hidden lights come on, bathing the lift in a glow of colour. Although this is just the sort of thing you have come to expect of this designer, the effect is still startling and titillating, leaving you with a definite sense of anticipation.

Unfortunately, you feel not so much invited into the main space as squeezed out of the vestibule and its slanted and oppressive, mahogany-faced walls. The space you end up in is immensely theatrical: completely glazed on three sides with dramatic 6-metre-high ceilings. You have no chance to take in your immediate surroundings, however, as your eye is instantly drawn to the oyster bar area at the back – a raised, glass-floored stage whose main prop is a 5-metre-long table made of thin sheets of alabaster on die-cast aluminium legs. Behind, a mesmerising curved aluminium wall is animated by a rippling light effect made by slashes in the metal surface. The message of 'look but don't touch' is overpowering. Although Starck himself has derided the city of Hong Kong for being 'a big cash register', this interior is just as guilty as the others. The space is appealing yet somehow maddeningly uninviting – a feeling heightened by the vigilant staff who over-reacted at the sight of a dictaphone. Floor-to-ceiling mahogany Venetian blinds partly block the spectacular view – as if the bar were jealously guarding the attention of its clientele.

As you have not yet dared to enter the main space, shimmy instead up the spiralling illuminated stairs of a monster pair of zinc buckets. These are clad in aluminium sheets and sheathed in camp, boudoir-like semi-translucent pleated curtains. Hidden within their frills is the green velvet space of the caviar bar. Beneath this is a wine bar with semicircular

Philippe Starck 1995

Tsim Sha Tsui

Phillipe Starck 1995

benches with a basket-weave backing. Walls are lined with horizontally arranged wine bottles. The other bucket contains an American-style bar in pink marble, aluminium and alabaster. Beneath this is the world's smallest disco (maximum five people), upholstered in a diamond-shaped padded quilt. Its curious, colourfully illuminated, curved cone stools have a rippling pattern similar to that on the oyster bar wall.

Other highlights include the beautifully finished mahogany column pieces (with a slightly colonial air) built to hide the building's pilasters. These bulge out to house the cashier's desk in the lower section. Silk-screened portraits of Starck's (top 100) friends and collaborators on the backs of the seats represent the ultimate in self-promotion. For some reason they are reminiscent of the playing card people in *Alice in Wonderland* and a bit frightening in a child's nightmare kind of way – will they bite your back if you sit on them?

The toilets, of course, are what you have really come to see – and they do not disappoint. The white-marble and sandblasted glass spaces are most notable in the men's urinals. The positioning of these (overlooking the harbour in front of floor-to-ceiling glazing) is said to ensure a memorable experience. The communal sink looks like a solid table on which sit strange amorphous sculptures – the taps and hand-dryer. Water flows into an ever-so-slight depression in the marble. An undeniably graceful and sexy sink. JC

LOCATION Peninsula Hotel extension, Salisbury Road, Kowloon
CLIENT Michael Kadoorie, Le Patrondes Hotel Peninsula
CONTRACTOR Gammon HK
MTR Central
ACCESS open

Philippe Starck 1995

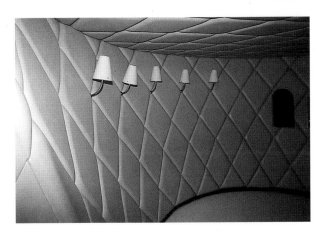

Philiipe Starck 1995

Parklane shopping boulevard

Nathan Road, long and straight with trees on both sides, was before 1985 a lifeless place with few facilities. But with the completion of the Parklane shopping boulevard, Rocco Design Partnership has given it a complete face lift: 370 metres of storefronts now line the eastern boundary of Kowloon Park and stretch from one end of Nathan Road to the other, making perhaps the longest building in Hong Kong.

The entire length of the strip is clad with snow-white aluminium panels. These give a fresh clean look and a definite edge to the park behind. At two points along its length the strip is interrupted by entrances into the park. The addition of postmodern motifs has dramatised these entrances and changed what were clean modern structures into something far less serious and more to do with very large Lego blocks (maybe they are trying to establish a connection with children in the park behind). Whatever, they now seem oddly out of place.

The long strip of shopfronts flanks a new pedestrian promenade where people can chat, linger, browse and enjoy the magnificent trees. It poses a strong urban presence and revitalises a previously sterile urban environment. AY

LOCATION RIL 10710, Nathan Road, Tsim Sha Tsui, Kowloon
SIZE 9000 square metres
COST HK$70 million
MTR Jordan
access open

Tsim Sha Tsui

Rocco Design Partnership 1985

Rocco Design Partnership 1985

Kowloon Park and indoor games complex

The most astonishing thing about Kowloon Park is its location. Situated just off the busiest section of Nathan Road, the mind boggles as to how much the 15-hectare site is worth as commercial property. Envisioned as a much-needed 'green lung' in the dense Tsim Sha Tsui area, the park, like many of Hong Kong's other surprisingly central public spaces, was previously a military encampment. In 1974 it was given to the Urban Council for development, but nothing happened until 1985 when the Royal Hong Kong Jockey Club decided to fund and project manage the park as part of its programme of community schemes. Derek Walker & Associates (in association with Simon Kwan & Associates) were asked to plan the development strategy for the park as well as the indoor games hall complex. The Urban Council may well have been swayed by Walker's grandiose quote: 'All men in their native powers are craftsmen whose destiny is to create a fit abiding place, a sane and beautiful world.'

Walker, previously chief architect and planner of Milton Keynes in England, had apparently not fully recovered from this experience, as is evident here, six years later. For example, one of the highlights of the park, the international sculpture court, stems from one of Walker's unsuccessful prize pursuits at Milton Keynes. His proposal for an international sculpture park and gallery there, despite being backed by many (including Henry Moore), had failed when money could not be raised following a change of government in Britain in 1979.

Kowloon Park is structured around a main north–south axial promenade (parallel to Nathan Road) which connects the entrance at Hoi Phong Road to the indoor sports complex. This is linked to numerous facilities by meandering pathways and bridges. In order to approximate as closely as possible the idyllic image of old and young going about their

Derek Walker & Associates/Simon Kwan & Associates Ltd 1989

Tsim Sha Tsui

leisure pursuits side by side, emphasis was placed on the division rather than sharing of space in order to accommodate the 100,000 people who use the park daily for a wide range of activities.

Kowloon Park provided Derek Walker Associates with a lesson in the interpretation of personal space. Residents of Hong Kong spend a lot of time outside their homes and often seek privacy in what elsewhere would be considered public space. Consequently, the different areas of the park were conceived as outdoor 'rooms', made private and isolated from each other by various landscape elements. Walker's love of landscape also results from an appetite whetted at Milton Keynes.

The Nathan Road entrance which breaks up the aptly named Shoppers Boulevard is sadly disappointing; with its gridded square columns of white enamel steel and strange pyramid-on-a-sphere object/sculpture, it would have been more apt as an entrance to a public toilet. A large flight of stairs and the lack of a decent view of the park from street level do not make it particularly inviting.

Once inside the park, however, there are plenty of things to see, hear and even smell. One of the best aspects of the park are the follies surrounding the Tai Chi garden, with stepped walkways covered by terracotta-coloured shingle roofs between them, and classic Chinese-shaped openings to peer into. Among the international artists featured in the open-air sculpture court are Paolozzi, Arnatt, Watkins, Van Lau and a changing group of Chinese Hong Kong and Pacific Basin sculptors. Other facilities include an outdoor arena, performance area and piazza; an aviary; an adventure playground; a viewing cone; a landmark fountain and various types of gardens; a fitness trail, a bird lake and a maze.

At first, the sports complex does not seem of any particular aesthetic interest. The coffered reinforced-concrete barrel-vault roof (over the

Tsim Sha Tsui

Derek Walker & Associates/Simon Kwan & Associates Ltd 1989

Tsim Sha Tsui

Derek Walker & Associates/Simon Kwan & Associates Ltd 1989

central axis entrance concourse) sits on precast tie-beams and spans the entire length of the building. A cross-axis leads to the Olympic-sized swimming pool complex on the right and sports halls on the left. The wide spans are of site-assembled, glazed-steel lattice construction. For the most part, the exterior is clad in white enamel steel panels.

There seems to be nothing exceptional here until you examine the historical references used. Walker has always looked to nineteenth-century glasshouse technology for inspiration; while a glasshouse was not appropriate in this climate, he still managed to achieve a feeling of light and transparency despite the predominantly solid opaque surfaces. The actual forms are neither beautiful nor awe-inspiring, but the natural white light, the glimpses of large expanses of water (off which sparkling reflections shimmer) and extensive greenery, together with the echoing sounds of water and people, do create a pleasing and appropriate atmosphere. It may not look especially good but somehow it feels good; the openness of the space is luxurious and inspiring, and it oozes health and fitness. External features include a Banyan court, soccer pitches and volleyball courts. There are also recreational, practice and diving pools. The outdoor swimming pool (which incorporates a paddling pool) is framed by artificial rock-like formations (a bit Flintstoney) with gradually sloping edges that mimic a natural beach. Though the previous quote may not have been fulfilled here, this one is perhaps more fitting: 'An architect is a man who can do for one dollar what any fool can do for two.' JC

ADDRESS 22 Austin Road
CLIENT Hong Kong Urban Council
MTR Tsim Sha Tsui or Jordan
ACCESS open

Tsim Sha Tsui

Derek Walker & Associates/Simon Kwan & Associates Ltd 1989

Hong Kong Science Museum

This project was conceived not only as a space in which to house exhibits but as an actual exhibit itself. Apart from the exhibition hall, the design of the 27,000-square-metre site has been imaginatively developed to present some of the themes explored inside the museum. The building design is based on an 'urban living room' concept. The site is divided into an upper and lower piazza, joined by a staircase which extends almost the entire width. The stairs, which double as a seating area, have a jagged waterfall carved into them. Water from the upper piazza's fountain flows down to the water feature of the lower piazza. The two levels are also connected by a pedestrian bridge which stretches out towards the east end of the site and then descends in a gracefully spiralling ramp.

The lower piazza is divided into two: the south section is a drop-off area for visitors arriving by car; the north section contains a multilateral structure with a lopsided figure-of-eight pattern in the middle. This is, in fact, a sundial, read by the shadow cast on to the pattern by a small ball attached to a pole. The marked gradations reveal not only the date but also whether the day falls on one of the 24 solar terms in the Chinese almanac. This elegant structure, which also serves to illustrate different aspects of our solar system (such as the Earth's elliptical orbit), makes use of a real – and free – element (sunlight) and is in marked contrast to the scaled-down models used almost exclusively inside the museum.

Other outdoor exhibits/structures include an echo wall, a pool with lighting which responds to surrounding sound frequencies, a tower with a dish-like antenna for receiving satellite signals which are then transmitted as images on to the screen in the Meteorology Hall, and a rectangular pool which uses optical fibres to add colour patterns to the water.

The four-storey-high museum provides 6500 square metres of exhibition space, including a special exhibitions hall, a 295-seat lecture hall, a

Tsim Sha Tsui

P & T Architects & Engineers Ltd 1990

Tsim Sha Tsui

P & T Architects & Engineers Ltd 1990

212 Hong Kong Science Museum

computer room, laboratory, classroom, gift shop and snack bar. Structurally the building is formed by a number of three-dimensional and geometrical forms clad in pink wall tiles. The more or less rectangular space which it occupies is delineated by a turquoise frame. Grey pillars and beams indicate the flexible planning grid on which the museum is based. It can be expanded and modified, according to the number and type of exhibition areas required, without any major structural changes.

A glazed space-frame arch with a protruding semicircular stainless-steel ring marks the entrance. Once inside you are greeted by the 22-metre-high Energy Machine which takes up almost the full height of the atrium space. Different parts of this kinetic sculpture (which describes the principles of energy conversion) can be viewed from each of the four floors. The enclosing balustrade is glass with fat tubular steel handrails to allow shorter visitors a good view too. Each floor is essentially an open space subdivided only by low or transparent walls or the exhibits themselves, encouraging visitors to wander freely between whatever catches their eye. JC

ADDRESS 2 Science Museum Road
CLIENT Hong Kong Urban Council
MTR Tsim Sha Tsui or Jordan
ACCESS Tuesday to Friday, 13.00–21.00; weekends and public holidays, 10.00–21.00 (17.00 on Lunar New Year's Eve and Christmas Eve); closed New Year's Day, the first three days of the Lunar New Year and Christmas Day

P & T Architects & Engineers Ltd 1990

Tsim Sha Tsui

P & T Architects & Engineers Ltd 1990

Grand Centre

The art deco Grand Hotel originally stood on this site. Its replacement comprises a three-level retail podium, a restaurant floor and 15 floors of executive office space (all with a highly marketable view of the harbour). The complex has been designed so that its height (and hence floor area) can be increased at a later date. The architects' intention was to enhance the building's corner location by emphasising the juxtaposition of the horizontal and vertical layering. With its streamlined curves in plan, the retail podium has a definite art deco feel. The horizontal lines whipping around the corner are accentuated at night by neon lighting in the detailed curtain-walling system. The podium façade also features a series of light boxes reminiscent of the buildings in art deco graphics.

The curtain wall extends up to the roof and works well in visually connecting the different parts of the building, whose various levels are physically linked by two-way glass elevators. In a clever reworking of an art deco theme, strongly detailed mullion and transom design features frame the large windows of this 1990s high-tech chrome structure.

The concave façade of the office block facing Carnarvon Road is elegantly curved with its edges gently peeling away from the main structure to add a certain grace and depth. This fin-like layer is echoed by a horizontally curved panel which arches over and conceals the otherwise unsightly rooftop elements and ancillary plant units. JC

ADDRESS 8 Humphreys Avenue
STRUCTURAL ENGINEER Ho Tin and Associates
CONTRACTOR Nishimatsu Construction Company Ltd
SIZE 10,896 square metres
MTR Tsim Sha Tsui
ACCESS open

Tsim Sha Tsui

Liang Peddle Thorp Architects/Kohn Pedersen Fox 1995

Liang Peddle Thorp Architects/Kohn Pederson Fox 1995

Golden Gateway Multiplex

A solid black rectangular archway frames a pair of double-glazed doors. The archway itself is in turn framed by a fully glazed façade which gives an open view into the cinema foyer. Between showings the space buzzes with people and, with the concession bar in full view, has more of a bar or club atmosphere and is extremely inviting from the outside.

The black protruding block on the right houses a ticket booth and a four-screen display which can be viewed from both the foyer and outside. The structure is angled so that a third, plain black façade leads the eye effectively towards the viewing theatres at the back.

The concession bar and the wheelchair ramp together form one element, divided by a rectangular-gridded wall of frosted glass panes. Two large overlapping circular lights which are projected on to this wall (to illuminate the ramp space behind and highlight the screen numbers) produce a peculiar optical illusion: because of their circular form and size you assume they must be from a far-off spotlight. This lends a dynamic quality to the area and a spooky feeling that a wall somewhere behind you has receded and the space has grown!

Reciprocal light sources (in black boxes above the ramped space) project back into the foyer space making the individual panes of glass look like lightboxes. In fact, a lot of things here look like lightboxes – from the white stairs to the rectangular translucent pieces which float just below the ceiling. The interiors of the cinemas are in various shades of the same purplish mauve colour. JC

ADDRESS 25 Canton Road
CONTRACTOR E-Pont Interiors Ltd
MTR Tsim Sha Tsui
ACCESS open

Wong & Choy Architecture 1995

Wong & Choy Architecture 1995

Majestic Cinema

Tucked behind Majestic Plaza is a stylish cinema entrance. The tall linear structure above (three storeys high) gives a hint of how far you must go to reach your seat.

The ground-floor ticket booth is situated on a narrow strip which also serves as a hallway. Above it, a wall of copper sheeting stretches up to the second storey, with roughly polished stainless-steel uplights defining the extent of this void (since there are spotlights underneath the transome adjacent to these lights and downlights on the ceiling, it is difficult to see any other reason why they are there).

Walls inside the cinema are covered with different sorts of perforated metal and sintered aluminium acoustic skins. According to the architects, the extensive use of metal sheets was a result of their investigation into 'the notion of skin and geometry', with the external copper wall 'slicing through space and time as an ever-changing sign'. AY

Tsim Sha Tsui

ADDRESS 48 Jordan Road, Jordan
SIZE 500 square metres
MRT Jordan
ACCESS open

Wong & Choy Architecture 1992

Tsim Sha Tsui

Wong & Choy Architecture 1992

North and East Kowloon

Hong Kong Productivity Council

The soft greys and matt metallics of the exterior are an indication of the general relaxed mood of the building, especially when compared with the high-tech industrial greys and shiny chrome used extensively in the previous decade. The metalwork (fine tubular sections and perforated panels) is no longer chunky, but lighter and more delicate. Its aesthetic is closer to that of, say, electronic components than heavy industrial machinery. Although some services are revealed, such as the group of three stacks near the entrance, they do not overpower. These structures, in fact, complement the front façade whereas previously they might have dominated aggressively. An effort at energy efficiency has been made by employing passive cooling techniques (restricted window openings and metal sunshades on both the south- and west-facing elevations) to reduce solar heat gain. The exterior is mainly clad in flat, square grey tiles.

This building provides 25,000 square metres for both training and research facilities. Besides a considerable amount of office space for administration, there are also workshops, laboratories, lecture theatres, classrooms, exhibition spaces and special function areas. Although all of these could have been housed in a standard office block, it is not surprising that a council devoted to the study of productivity should favour a building uniquely tailored to its special needs.

In plan, the building is strangely shaped. This is due partly to the physical constraints of the site – an irregular-shaped plot and a drainage reserve placed restrictions on land coverage – and partly to a shift in priorities in the project brief. The challenge here was to give shape to the required functions rather than fitting the functions into a designated shape. Not an unusual idea, you might think, but it is when placed in the context of Hong Kong where the first priority is almost always to squeeze the maximum floor area out of a site and then to see what fits. Problems

Simon Kwan & Associates Ltd 1990

Simon Kwan & Associates Ltd 1990

of noise and vibration also had to be taken into account as the site is close to a KCR/MTR station and in the Kai Tak runway approach flight path.

You can sense immediately that one of the major concerns of this project was to design a 'productive work environment'. This is not to say it has a treadmill-like atmosphere. Quite the opposite, in fact. As you enter the foyer of the building with its combination of natural light and soothing subdued artificial lighting, you feel a strong sense of contrived comfort. Someone definitely had in mind that 'a happy relaxed worker equals a good productive worker'. It soon becomes apparent that a great deal of thought has gone into these areas because they do create a very relaxed atmosphere. Sitting in the pleasant plant-filled central light-court – a peaceful 'dark' light-court! – you can almost feel the incoming power surge as your personal battery recharger is switched on (a hard seating surface ensures you won't overcharge). This semicircular light-court is enclosed by the glass elevators and staircase on one side and office spaces and walkways on the other. The gaps on each floor which overlook the light-court are left open and unglazed.

The only slight problem here is that you might be overwhelmed by the feeling that you are unwittingly taking part in some sort of environmental experiment. This may lead to paranoid guessing games in which you start wondering about the employment of each and every design detail. For example, did they actually work out whether matt or shiny grey marble would be the most relaxing/energising material for the floor? JC

ADDRESS 76 Tat Choo Avenue, Kowloon Tong
CLIENT Hong Kong Productivity Council
MTR Kowloon Tong
ACCESS open

Simon Kwan & Associates Ltd 1990

Simon Kwan & Associates Ltd 1990

Lok Fu shopping centre II

This large seven-storey extension to an existing shopping centre within a low-cost public housing estate also serves as a traffic interchange. It provides more than 10,000 square metres of retail, cinema and restaurant space, together with public car parking. Although the many different levels make the site extremely complex, Rocco Design Partners have successfully imposed a multi-storey skylit atrium to create a striking spatial reference. This void serves as a breathing space between the transport interchange and pedestrian traffic. Cinemas, restaurants and the link to the older shopping complex are all on the top level.

What makes Lok Fu stand out from other shopping complexes is the structure itself, not the retail units within. The building is both simple and refined. Structural elements and services are boldly and consistently expressed and can be read as coherent components against the chaos of shopfronts and pedestrian movement. This spatial clarity helps to move people through the building without having to rely heavily on signage. The centre thus not only provides a solution to the problem of pedestrian traffic, but elevates what is normally a routine and mundane exercise to an uplifting urban experience.

In front of the building is a large open space, partly sheltered and provided with seats. It is difficult to find such generous and pleasant spaces within commercial developments in the city centre. AY

ADDRESS Wang Tau Hum East Road, Junction Road, Kowloon
CLIENT Hong Kong Housing Authority
STRUCTURAL ENGINEER Harris & Sutherland Ltd
COST HK$200 million
MTR Lok Fu
ACCESS open

North and East Kowloon

Rocco Design Partnership 1991

Rocco Design Partnership 1991

Dragon Centre (East Kowloon Centre)

Just when you think you have seen every possible configuration of shopping complex, this arcade with nine floors of retail units and restaurants around an elliptical glazed atrium will make you think again. On the eighth floor, just below the glass roof, is an entertainment centre featuring an electronic arcade, an ice-skating rink and an indoor rollercoaster ride, with bright yellow tracks running frantically across the atrium.

The 45,000-square-metre commercial portion evolves around the central atrium. To keep this vertical mall vibrant throughout, *di pia dong* (traditional fast-food-style) restaurants are set up on the eighth floor, together with the scattered elements of the entertainment centre. You may find yourself eating right next to the ice-skating rink with the mini roller coaster running just above your head. The whole floor feels more like a playing field than a shopping mall.

To encourage customers to go up to the higher levels, a dominant lift tower is placed in the atrium. Overly dramatic lift lobbies with translucent acrylic panels and blue tinted lights on floor and ceiling are repeated on each level. Escalators are located directly behind the full-height glass wall which echoes the elliptical atrium on the front elevation. A skip-floor system provides rapid access to the upper floors.

Much of the ground floor is occupied by a public transport terminus. Being situated in the Sham Shui Po area, the building was subject to a height restriction determined by air traffic movement. The huge floor space requirement for vehicles was achieved by creating five basement floors of loading areas and parking space for both private cars and trucks, making this the deepest basement in Hong Kong.

Dragon Centre is an investment in a much-neglected part of the Sham Shui Po area. The whole complex is vibrant and playful. A successful re-invention of public space makes Dragon Centre a more exciting place

Wong Tung & Partners Ltd 1994

Wong Tung & Partners Ltd 1994

than most podiums in Central. Although the architecture of the complex is inconsistent, and in some areas the detail is clumsy, the building succeeds on a level that is both experimental and bold. AY

North and East Kowloon

LOCATION Sham Shui Po, Kowloon
COST HK$800 million
MTR Sham Shui Po
ACCESS open

Wong Tung & Partners Ltd 1994

Wong Tung & Partners Ltd 1994

Chan residence

This breathtaking private residence on a hilltop site was originally a characteristic 1950s modern town house with a private garden. Due to flight path restrictions, streets and houses on Kadoorie Hill have not changed dramatically. The area has the quality of a 1950s black-and-white film set and, despite its proximity to Kai Tak airport, is surprisingly quiet.

The architect has transformed the building by introducing new components and materials while preserving the spatial quality of the original. The structure was stripped back to its skeleton and, where applicable, a steel glazing system was introduced to increase transparency and let in more light. Every detail is obsessively thought out and beautifully crafted. Chan has explored modernist themes here, but there is also more than a hint of international-style minimalism. Spatial expression has undoubtedly a strong Chinese influence. The resultant mix is extraordinary.

Entry into the house reveals a series of interconnected living spaces, screened by sliding wooden panels to cope with different family activities. The kitchen, as in a conventional Chinese house, is hidden from the dinning area.

There is an intrinsic relationship between the inside and the outside. On the exterior, limestone cladding is strategically placed to blur the distinction, and timber decks match the internal floor level and successfully create an intermediate zone between the house and the garden. AY

LOCATION Kadoorie Hill, Kowloon
CLIENTS Enrique and Ann Chan
CONTRACTOR Kuen Lee Decoration Co. Ltd
COST HK$7.02 million
MTR Kowloon Bay
ACCESS none

North and East Kowloon

Norman Chan 1994

Norman Chan 1994

Kowloon Bay training centre

It is not the centre itself which is notable but the buildings within it.

If you take the MTR between Kowloon Bay and Ngau Tau Kok, look to the right and you will see what at first appears to be a small construction site. There will probably be a small structure engulfed in bamboo scaffolding with many builders busily working away on it. It looks to be an extension of some sort to the two larger adjacent buildings which together form a c-shaped plan. However, if you make the same journey repeatedly you will notice that just when the building seems to be nearing completion it disappears! What you are seeing is, in fact, a practical training exercise by building apprentices. In the courtyard of the school, a real (to scale) building is erected and then torn down in order to be started again. It would be frighteningly reminiscent of Hades (although there is no sign of anyone eternally pushing a large boulder up a hill) if it did not make such perfectly good sense – learn to build by erecting practice structures. If you look through the large windows of the main building you will see little brick walls being constructed in the middle of vast interior spaces. JC

ADDRESS 46 Tai Yip Street, Kowlloon (between Kowloon Bay and Ngau Tau Kok MTR stations)
MTR Kowloon Bay
ACCESS limited

David Ho & Partners 1984

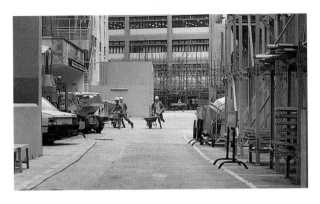

David Ho & Partners 1984

Sha Tin

Kwong Yuen housing estate

The Housing Department Construction Branch (of the Hong Kong housing authority) started out as a small office of 130 staff in the early 1970s and has since grown to a multi-disciplinary organisation of 3200 whose responsibilities include all aspects of housing design, construction and maintenance. Its main objective is to deal with the ever-increasing demand for affordable housing. By 1994 it had built 600,000 flats, and is scheduled to complete another 400,000 by the year 2000. A budget of US$6 billion has been allocated for the construction of these new estates and for the maintenance of existing buildings (including over 1.2 million square metres of commercial space, 600 schools, flatted factories and numerous welfare and recreational facilities). While these figures are not proof of success, they do nonetheless show that these housing estates are a workable solution.

In order to appreciate this particular estate, you need to place it in context by visiting a few others. Unless you are familiar with the type, it is all too easy to look at an isolated example and criticise it for something that is inherent within the whole genre of standardised buildings in high-density developments. It is important not to overlook the fact that the main concern is to meet the urgent need for housing, coupled with the scarce resource of land.

The Kwong Yuen housing estate is significant for the way it has achieved the all-too-elusive 'sense of community' sought by generation after generation of housing-estate architects. Built by the housing authority and private developers, this estate comprises 12 housing blocks providing 8000 flats, two primary schools, a community centre, two car park buildings, a bus terminal, shopping and market facilities, restaurants (surprisingly crowded when we visited for a weekday dim sum) and, of course, communal open spaces. The 12.5-hectare site lies in a confined

Sha Tin

Housing Department Construction Branch 1991

Sha Tin

Housing Department Construction Branch 1991

east–west oriented valley and has views of the Shing Mun river. The estate has a total population of 30,000 – a density of 2400 people per hectare, which is fairly typical of current public housing projects.

What is surprising and refreshing about Kwong Yuen is the design of its central public areas. The tall domestic blocks are arranged in a crescent to the south and west of the central area. Here, rather than the predictable multi-storey podium mall, a cluster of five two-storey buildings on different levels mimic the layout of a Chinese hillside village. The centre is traffic-free and service roads are confined to the western perimeter. The forms of the buildings are fluid and graceful yet unpretentious and comfortable. Although the same natural earthy colours are used throughout, the circulation areas, semi-enclosed spaces, covered walkways and seating areas are distinguished by different tiles and tiling patterns on the ground. Most of the buildings are clad in shiny brick-coloured tile except for the covered walkway of grey-dotted-with-yellow mosaic tiles and the little parking attendant structure in brown-and-green mosaic tiles. Without a restrictive grid layout, the paths seem more interesting and there is a certain sense of serendipity as the winding paths and stairs lead to a number of special features, such as the sheltered Chinese chess table. There is, however, a slightly artificial air (could it be the incongruous pairing of a traditional, pitched Chinese roof and curved tiles with a post-modern broken pediment?) or theatricality about the place which brings to mind one of Kurosawa's Japanese-village film sets.

A series of courtyards is linked by gently curved ramps and short flights of stairs. The layout of the main steps and zig-zagging ramps forms teardrop-shaped bedding areas reminiscent of a Burle Marx plan. The trees and shrubs look especially lush and well tended – in contrast to the empty and neglected flower beds often seen on the housing estates of Britain.

Sha Tin

Housing Department Construction Branch 1991

Sha Tin

Housing Department Construction Branch 1991

The vegetation is slightly overgrown in parts and occasionally tumbles over low walls on to seating areas and steps – yet this only imparts a more relaxed atmosphere and saves the estate from the dangers of being too Stepford-like. Overall, the estate with its meandering pathways and plentiful seating and rest areas has a very relaxed atmosphere.

The success which this housing estate has achieved with its much sought-after 'outdoor living-room' concept is immediately apparent when you visit the site and see children, grandmas and granddads, teenagers and young couples all strolling around or simply hanging about. The scene verges on the idyllic – an urban planning fantasy. These people are the real-life versions of those figures in architects' presentation perspectives – the ones who often look suspiciously elated at the prospect of being in the soon-to-be-built 'piazzas' and yet never seem to materialise in the built version.

The focal point of the whole scheme is a 26-metre-high clocktower. Serving as a landmark and meeting point, it signifies the many hectic work schedules that coexist here. JC

Sha Tin

ADDRESS adjacent to Tate's Cairn Highway
KCR Sha Tin
BUS 49X, 82M, 83X
ACCESS public areas open

Housing Department Construction Branch 1991

Sha Tin

Housing Department Construction Branch 1991

Bo Fook Hill

You might be forgiven for thinking that you have just entered a life-size replica of Noah's ark (you are repeatedly greeted by pairs of animals – two roaring stone lions, a pair of stone camels and a pair of bowing elephants) until, that is, you reach a pair of incense burners and, later, a pair of dragons. This is not a biblical theme park but a Chinese/Buddhist columbarium which just happens to have a symmetrical theme at its entrance. Actually it is half public park, half preserve for cinerary urns. It is situated beside the Ten Thousand Buddhas Monastery, and Bo Fook itself means 'precious luck'.

The first half of the site is supposedly landscaped like a traditional Chinese garden, yet unfortunately it is also reminiscent of a miniature golf course with stone bridges, rocks representing mountains, water cascades and a tortoise pool. There is a statue of Wu Lan, and mosaic tiles of a four-faced god, as well as other typical symbols from Chinese imagery such as flowers and birds. The steep incline to the various pavilions is accessed by a series of covered escalators clad in green tiles. Further pairs of animal statues greet you at each level. A wooden diagonal lift with seats provides an alternative, quicker route to the top of the site (and the main worship hall) for the elderly, infirm or just plain lazy. The ride allows equally impressive views of Sha Tin as the slower walk up. Incidentally, only flowers and vegetarian food are allowed in the halls.

The series of green-roofed Chinese-style buildings have a distinctive bright red framework set against a white façade and, oddly, look rather like beach huts from afar. An air of tranquillity is felt immediately you step under the shaded patio area into the main worship hall. The high ceiling is emphasised by bright blue and turquoise and red-striped rafters. This building, together with the (octagonal in plan) pagoda, houses a total of four camphor-wood Buddhas covered in gold leaf. Some of the struc-

Chung Wah Nan Partners 1990

Chung Wah Nan Partners 1990

Sha Tin

tures have gold roofs festooned with brightly coloured lightbulbs. All together this Tang dynasty-style complex covers 200,000 square metres and is the final resting place for the remains of 40,000 people.

Two stories told about this project give a good indication of the extent of issues involved in an average Hong Kong architect's plan of work. Apparently, halfway through completion, the client wanted to relocate the pagoda to the front of the courtyard area of the main hall, but the architect refused. Surprisingly, the client congratulated the architect at the opening ceremony. This was only because he had secretly consulted a feng shui practitioner who declared that the pagoda was sitting on a 'Chien' position – in other words, in the best possible location. The other story involved the positioning of the Buddha in the pagoda. When the architect requested the contractor to move the statue on to the centre line, the foreman explained that they had tried to, but the statue had moved itself back each time. And this is where it remains today. JC

ADDRESS Lot 311, Pau Tau Street
CLIENT China Overseas Building Development Co. Ltd
KCR walk from Sha Tin station
ACCESS open 9.00–17.00 daily

Sha Tin

Chung Wah Nan Partners 1990

Chung Wah Nan Partners 1990

Treasure floating restaurant

A real misnomer here as this building is neither floating nor much of a treasure. It does highlight a few interesting ironies, though. A large part of Sha Tin comprises reclaimed land filled in with material taken from the adjoining hillsides. To place a pseudo-floating structure in what has been chosen to be left as 'sea' (Shing Mun river) is somewhat incongruous and verging on the absurd. 'Firmly docked' (in the Hong Kong Tourist Authority's words), it sits on a concrete base in impossibly shallow water. No one could be fooled into thinking this structure could set off on a sojourn down the river; it is no more floating than the rest of Sha Tin. It yearns to be Sha Tin New Town's very own version of Beijing's floating palace, with a VIP seafood lounge and its own mooncakes during the mid-autumn festival.

Unfortunately, the style of the restaurant is more or less that of other 'treasures' found in Chinatowns all around the world. Indistinguishably clad in grey tiles with dark pinkish-red awnings, the three-decked structure can only be described as confused. With the huge housing estate of Sha Tin New Town as a backdrop, the building seems surprisingly unself-conscious about being the oddity it truly is.

The scale of some details, borrowed from traditional Chinese forms, is at odds not only with the surroundings but with the building itself. Relief sculptures (of the four beauties – a popular subject in Chinese figurative art) in brown stone and mosaic adorn the four corner turrets, which are topped by ineffectual little pitched roofs. White stone walkways and bridges lead to the building from the land, awkwardly disrupting any delusions of it being a boat.

A multitude of variously sized fish – all exactly the same dirty brown colour as the water – scavenge around the base of the building. You are forced to contrast their muddy happy lives with the fish swimming (well,

Sha Tin

architect and date unknown

architect and date unknown

squirming) inside the large tank which greets you in the entrance lobby of the restaurant. Apparently it contains enough fish to make a tasty meal for up to 2400 people. If those on the outside only knew what was happening in here, perhaps even now they would be planning the construction of an escape tunnel connecting the tanks to Shing Mun river.
JC

Sha Tin

ADDRESS Sha Tin New Town waterfront
KCR Sha Tin
ACCESS open

architect and date unknown

Sha Tin

architect and date unknown

Church of St Benedict

Sites for new church development are obtained through the Lands Department of the Hong Kong government. They vary in size from a few thousand to approximately 10,000 square metres.

The church of St Benedict is situated amongst the housing blocks of a new town. This rectangular box – a plain and rigorous composition clad in light-grey stone tiles – is as sophisticated as it is stylish, with purist and modernist themes revealing the signature of the architect. As in many churches, a peaceful calmness occupies the interior, which has simple wooden furniture and a suspended ceiling. It is lit by full-height stained-glass windows, and a narrow slit of rooflight above the altar emphasises the importance of this particular space.

The triple-height internal front court, flooded with natural light from the roof garden above, is institutional yet inviting. AY

ADDRESS STTL 285, area 5B,
Kong Pui Street, Sha Tin
SITE AREA 7230 square metres
KCR Sha Tin
ACCESS open

Anthony K K Ng with KNW Architects & Engineers Ltd 1988

Sha Tin

Anthony K K Ng with KNW Architects & Engineers Ltd 1988

Ho Sin Hang engineering building

Eleven storeys high and surrounded by mature trees, this bold new engineering block stands out from the other university departments lower down on campus. From a distance it is like a giant building frame with large mechanical fixing parts at the corner of each panel. Solid and open modules within these slots look as if they could be rearranged at will. And the objective of Tao Ho's design was indeed to create maximum flexibility so that different functions could be slotted in and out as the technology and requirements of the engineering faculty developed. This aim, however, did not progress beyond the conceptual stage and is merely hinted at on the surface of the building. What, in fact, from a distance look like mechanical fixings are only decorative pieces. And the rooms are not in prefabricated units so they cannot physically be relocated.

There is not much detail to look at since mosaic tiles cover virtually every surface, both inside and out. The building's 'book-shelf' modularity is reflected in the interiors, where the accentuated colour scheme of the framework makes for an interesting composition. The sixth-floor link bridge and open space make an impressive feature and help to bring the exterior into the building.

Overall, the design works well, both on the campus as a whole and as a department building, with plenty of informal meeting places. The structure and volume of the building are clearly expressed, making it particularly interesting to view from a distance. AY

LOCATION The Chinese University, Sha Tin
GROSS FLOOR AREA 19,150 square metres
COST HK$105 million
KCR University
ACCESS limited

Sha Tin

Tao Ho Design Architects 1994

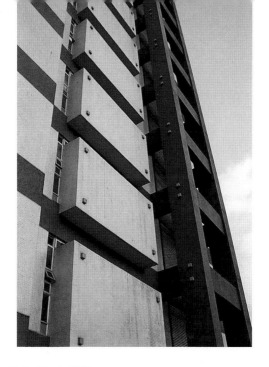

Sha Tin

Tao Ho Design Architects 1994

Others

Tsuen Wan Columbarium

The people of Hong Kong have a deep reverence for their ancestors. Each spring and autumn thousands pay their respects at the Ching Ming and Chung Yeung festivals. Due to the shortage of land, cremation is promoted by the government, although there are still a number of large cemeteries operated by state and private organisations.

The Columbarium is a long, thin, ten-storey structure situated on one of the many existing terraces within Tsuen Wan Chinese Permanent Cemetery. Its cantilevered floors with greenery entrwined among the balustrades are a successful re-interpretation of these terraces. The lowest three levels contain 36 rooms for 1925 'family' niches. The remaining seven levels provide 26,060 'ordinary' niches, with a capacity for 60,004 sets of ashes. On completion of the Columbarium in 1987, a family niche sold for HK$13,800, while an ordinary niche cost HK$1500.

The six-storey skylit central atrium acts as a unifying element in the design. From it the horizontal wings of the multi-storey structure extend to the left and the right, both above and below the entrance level. Adjoining the atrium is a pair of 20-metre-high stone murals with religious figures and a 'World of Perfect Happiness' theme. The entrance creates an ambience of serenity, yet not of the sombre and uneasy kind normally associated with burial grounds. AY

LOCATION Lot 295 in DD446, Tsuen Wan, Kowloon
SITE AREA 11,247 square metres
GROSS FLOOR AREA 22,293 square metres
COST HK$30 million
MTR Kwai Fong
BUS 44
ACCESS open

Others

Dennis Lau & Ng Chen Man 1987

ALT freight container station

With a floor area of approximately 280,000 square metres in phases 1 and 2, this container station is one of the world's largest industrial buildings. The design of the building is to a great extent determined by the movement of incoming and outgoing containers. Freight areas at both ends of the rectangular building are served by parking spaces, reached via a drive-up ramp structure. A 16-storey-high space is designed to take four containers stacked vertically. Almost all of the ground floor is taken up with stacked containers, and the columns are spaced to accommodate the operation of the bridge crane which moves them around.

One of the most interesting aspects of the building is the multi-lane vehicle ramp which allows rapid access to all six levels and the roof, bypassing the loading and unloading traffic. With this ramp the upper levels of the building are just as accessible as the ground floor. AY

LOCATION Kwai Chung Berth 3, K C L 3, New Territories
SITE AREA Phase 1 & 2 279,000 square metres; Phase 3, 4 & 5 536,000
COST HK$3 million
ACCESS none2

Others

Dennis Lau & Ng Chen Man 1992

Others

Dennis Lau & Ng Chen Man 1992

Star TV broadcasting centre

This building is the headquarters of the first satellite television station in Hong Kong and houses both the production and administration facilities. On the approach to the building, because there are no signs, no big welcoming billboards, you get the feeling that this is a very private compound with an almost secret-service kind of atmosphere. The site is extremely remote by Hong Kong standards and sits on the edge of a hill overlooking a sparsely built-up valley. The lack of people – and of that certain sense of security that comes from being part of a Hong Kong city crowd – leaves a disconcerting feeling. Suddenly there is all this space and it is this feeling of being left alone which draws you towards the entrance – to look for others. The enclosing wall and security guard, however, make you feel like an intruder before you even get close.

The main entrance itself is set back. Although the lobby space within is perfectly visible through the double-height glazed façade, there is still no sign of anyone. On the right of the lobby is a square box with a large triangular skylight space sitting above it, and on the left is a rectangular wing with a curved ceiling and in front a frame-like structure running along its length. Behind the lobby is the main three-storey mass, divided into different blocks so as to provide a more human scale. Unfortunately, the different elements still seem vastly over-scaled, and a lack of familiar components such as handrails or standard sill heights only increases this impression. Most of the parts are clad in a nondescript pale-grey tile.

The pleasant circular drive in front is the first welcoming sign. As the ground level of the site is uniform to match the lowest point, the area you first see is quite deeply set into the ground, and high walls were needed to separate it from the neighbouring site. The encompassing whiteness of everything here makes it look like a sterile vacuum (where a speck of dust might interfere with the job at hand). It is a scene from a science-

Dennis Lau & Ng Chen Man 1991

Dennis Lau & Ng Chen Man 1991

fiction fantasy of a highly technical and distant world; you half expect people in white space suits to come out and tinker with the mechanisms.

The real facilities housed within the 4645 square metres of floor space are two production studios with a box-in-box structure; a scenery dock; editing, production and dubbing suites; administrative offices; conference rooms; a cafeteria; and up- and downlinking satellite facilities.

The key here is that the huge satellite dishes are the main medium of transport here, the link to the outside world. Over our heads, information and images fly off at great speeds to distant destinations – and the building shows no desire to, and hence does not, work at a mere pedestrian level.

The building received an award from the Hong Kong Institute of Architects in 1994. JC

ADDRESS Lot 830 in DD225, Sheung Yeung, Clearwater Bay Road, Sai Kung
CLIENT Satellite Television Asian Region Ltd
SIZE 9290 square metres
MTR Choi Hung, then take a taxi or bus 91
ACCESS none

Others

Dennis Lau & Ng Chen Man 1991

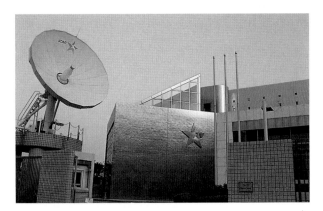

Dennis Lau & Ng Chen Man 1991

Hong Kong University of Science and Technology

Occupying a 60-hectare site at Clearwater Bay Peninsula, this university campus for 7000 students (eventually increasing to 10,000) needed to be designed, built and opened (in phases) in less than four years. The most spectacular aspect of the project is the site itself, with a cross-level drop of 125 metres over 500 metres. Although the campus makes use of the platforms, roads and basic utilities built by Ove Arup for the previous occupant of the site, Kohima Barracks, many difficult structural issues had to be overcome, some platforms needed to be enlarged and additional service roads were required. The original brief for the two-stage architectural competition called for the creation of 'a total, comprehensive environment … [which] may be seen as a living organism which adapts to rapid changes in technology, provides a visual impression of experiment and enquiry, and is both functional and aesthetically pleasing'. Remarkably, this demanding brief has been more or less fulfilled.

Although it does not literally look like a living organism, the organisation of the site does resemble one. A core mass of key buildings sits on the main axis of the campus, with limb-like extensions to the other built elements. The proximity of the different parts (the university comprises four schools with 19 departments) has been well co-ordinated, with frequently used routes taking priority over others. Since many facilities are shared between different departments, the main academic areas are placed together in a compact form, leaving the shoreline and outlying areas for residential and sports facilities. The design of the layout follows Simon Kwan & Associates' 'non-linear' approach to massing and form whereas, in contrast, the interiors result from the Percy Thomas Partnership's 'modular' style.

The overall design is made up of three basic motifs – a semicircle,

Percy Thomas Partnership/Simon Kwan & Associates 1991

Percy Thomas Partnership/Simon Kwan & Associates 1991

square and triangle. The simplicity of these forms allows the multitude of parts to be easily read and relatively free from confusion. But there is still a healthy complexity in the juxtaposition of forms for the geometric components, patterns and outlines range in size from tiny details to complete buildings. The main colour used is light grey, with red, yellow and blue accents.

At the main entrance is a huge curved concrete wall with square openings corresponding to the windows of the building behind. The curve radiates from a centre point which is marked by a red steel sundial. This 8-metre-high sculpture is intended to be symbolic of early technology and represents the ancient cultures of both east and west. Larger punched-out openings in the curved wall form archways leading to the main axis, where students can then head east to the housing and sports amenities or north and south to laboratories and classrooms.

The grand atrium, paved with granite cobblestones and topped by a vaulted skylight with a chunky red frame, provides space for exhibitions and other student activities. The mushroom-shaped opening at the far end gives a breathtaking view of Port Shelter and Pak Sha Wan. Students taking a break here between classes can gaze out at the distant blue mountains and feel the sea breeze on their faces, leaving them refreshed and in a contemplative mood. Lest they get too dizzy and emotional, the red and black tiles on the floor (like graph paper) serve as a gentle reminder of the scientific mind they are here to develop.

Other highlights include the middle pavilion which has a pointy skylight with rectangular openings framing postcard-perfect images of the surrounding scenery. One of the openings to the right gives a partial view of a small staircase which floats poetically over a hill, mimicking the irregular shape of a distant mountain. Also visible from these openings

Percy Thomas Partnership/Simon Kwan & Associates 1991

Percy Thomas Partnership/Simon Kwan & Associates 1991

are some of the other university buildings and their freestanding wall façades which throw dramatically sharp shadows on to their surroundings. A small sculpture garden which crops up in one of these shadows contains a work by Antonio Mok Ku entitled *Heaven and Hell*. This piece takes advantage of the view by reflecting the open sky at the bottom of a short flight of stairs dug into the ground. JC

LOCATION Clearwater Bay, Kowloon
STRUCTURAL ENGINEER Ove Arup & Partners
MTR Choi Hung, then take a taxi or bus (destination Hong Kong University of Science and Technology marked)
ACCESS open

Others

Percy Thomas Partnership/Simon Kwan & Associates 1991

Percy Thomas Partnership/Simon Kwan & Associates 1991

This fishing village in the far north-west of Lantau Island is entirely made up of aluminium stilt houses. With the picturesque landscape of drifting mist and blue-grey mountains as a backdrop, this community of shiny silver, box-like structures on stilts is unique, charming and decidedly eccentric. (It is said that its elevated architecture stems from the fact that Tanka boat people do not feel safe on land.)

The village (a Hong Kong Venice) is divided into three by narrow canals and the main transport is by small boats or sampans. Between the houses, narrow-planked pedestrian ramps span across the creeks and tidal waters below. The wooden paths meander and curve around the structures and other obstructions (a multitude of telegraph poles and electricity cables) in a seemingly organic growth pattern.

Although most houses have two floors, at low tide with the family boat parked beside the now fully visible ladder, they seem more like three-storey buildings. Windows are small and plain with green frames and glass of mismatched patterns. There are also openings with aluminium doors which can be propped open and which in turn support a horizontal door/awning. A third type of opening is a small door with an even smaller window in it. All three types have a beautiful simplicity to them.

Many of the terraces are crowded with lush potted plants and some are sagging dangerously under the weight. Household objects create colourful points of visual interest: filled laundry lines, plastic buckets and tubs, trolleys, stacked wicker baskets, old wooden stools, a yellow umbrella, a pink child's bicycle, a lifesaver and even household appliances all sit outside in the open – a good indication of how much of daily life here is spent outdoors.

The most memorable thing about the houses is the way the railings and platforms and their supportive structures have been constructed from

a combination of various pieces of wood, steel poles, mesh and basically whatever the owners could find. Even segments of proper railings (complete with handrails) salvaged from other buildings are worked into the fabric.

Small secondary structures can be found sitting on the terraces and attached to the sides of houses, jutting out over the water (sometimes with stilts of their own). These are in matching aluminium and some are covered in striped or checkered Chinese plastic material (seen everywhere, from carrier bags to coverings for whole buildings). Another structure extends outwards to make a simple rectangular frame on which a boat is dry-docked. Everything has a makeshift atmosphere yet somehow manages to look lived in and cheerful as well.

Other things to look out for in Tai O are an animist shrine (of prehistoric origin?) and a rope-drawn sampan ferry which is hauled across a creek by village women. JC

LOCATION Lantau Island
GETTING THERE from Central take the ferry to Mui Wo (an hour's ride) then take bus 1 (45-minute bus ride)

Others

Seated Buddha, Lantau

Because of this city's long-running love affair with (and indiscriminate overuse of) superlatives – biggest, tallest, smallest, smelliest – the phrase 'the largest seated Buddha' will probably elicit little more than a bored yawn. However, put away any such preconceptions and go and visit it. Climb up the long (longest to a seated Buddha?) stairs until you reach a choice position, such as underneath his raised hand. It is enormous. Impressively so. The sheer size of the whole structure is somehow profound. Its smallest details are probably the same size as your head.

The Buddha was built in Nanjing and assembled in Hong Kong. There are no visible seams and the weathered bronze material gives the sculpture a rich texture and solid presence.

The symbolic image of the Buddha is so often depicted as an object (even in 2D) and so firmly thought of as one, that you get a momentary feeling here that the Buddha is not big, but you are small. Somehow you have shrunk and are now able to walk under and around or perhaps climb on something you would normally hold in your hand. You are a modern-day Gulliver and not just a Hong Kong tourist. Of course, it helps that the atmosphere up here is quite thin.

The view is breathtaking and dreamy, making this an appropriate place to contemplate Zen doctrines. Say to yourself 'form is emptiness, emptiness is form' and feel the duality between subject and object dissolve away.

For the record, the Buddha weighs 202 tonnes and is 26 metres high – the tallest bronze sculpture in the world. JC

LOCATION Po Lin Monastery, Ngong Ping Plateau
GETTING THERE from Central take the ferry to Mui Wo (an hour's ride) then take bus (massive queue, destination Po Lin Monastery marked)
ACCESS open 10.00–16.00

Others

Department of Aviation Industry of China 1990

Department of Aviation Industry of China 1990

Future developments

Tsing Ma bridge

A major factor in Hong Kong's extraordinary recent growth has been its strategic location on the Asia-Pacific Rim, where it acts as a gateway to southern China. The volume of air and sea traffic has expanded rapidly during the past decade and a huge amount of money is being invested on urban infrastructure. This plan includes the new airport at Chek Lap Kok just off Lantau Island's northern coast (see page 284), and the concentration of new container-port berths around the island's north-eastern tip. Implementation of this plan has required construction on an unprecedented scale, including new high-capacity highway and railway systems.

The new Tsing Ma bridge spans the Ma Wan Channel (the only access for ocean-going ships to the ports upstream) between the islands of Tsing Yi and Ma Wan. This steel suspension bridge has a main span of 1377 metres – the longest combined road and rail span in the world – and a total length of 2160 metres.

The deck section uses double-deck box construction with truss stiffening and non-structural edge fairings. Longitudinal air vents are provided in the upper and lower surfaces to enhance stability.

The two anchorages are gravity structures which are integral with the deck abutments. At Tsing Yi the anchorage is largely below ground in a 290,000-cubic-metre rock excavation. In contrast, the Ma Wan anchorage is only partially buried. On Tsing Yi the layout of the highway in the side span is severely restricted by the adjacent steep hillsides. As deep water is close to the shore, the highway is required to diverge from the centre line of the bridge at the tower. This precludes the adoption of a suspended span and the approach therefore consists of four spans of 72 metres supported on voided reinforced-concrete piers. The Ma Wan tower is located in shallow water approximately 400 metres from the

Yee Associates and Mott MacDonald 1997

Yee Associates and Mott MacDonald 1997

original shoreline at the limit of relatively shallow water. However, it is set back from the navigation channel sufficiently to allow construction of an island to protect the bridge from stray ships. The suspended side span has a length of 355 metres.

The 206-metre-high reinforced-concrete towers were slipformed. Each tower leg is 6 metres wide and tapers from 18 to 9 metres in the longitudinal direction. The legs are inclined towards each other at a slope of 1 in 100. They are connected by deep prestressed concrete portal beams which resist sway forces. In order to stabilise the legs against possible high winds during construction, steel trusses were first installed at the portal locations. These trusses were subsequently encased within the permanent concrete beams.

As the only road and rail access to the new airport and port will initially be via the Tsing Ma bridge, it is vital that the bridge can continue to operate in all weather conditions. Two single-lane carriageways and the Airport Railway are located on the lower deck, protected by aerodynamic stainless steel cladding.

Construction started in May 1992 and the cable spinning was completed in the spring of 1995. The deck units have been assembled in China from components fabricated mainly in Britain and Japan. AY

Future developments

LOCATION between Tsing Yi and Ma Wan islands

Yee Associates and Mott MacDonald 1997

Yee Associates and Mott MacDonald 1997

Chek Lap Kok: airport terminal

This purpose-built airport island, located at Chek Lap Kok, will become number two in the short list of 'man-made objects seen from space' (after the Great Wall of China). The land reclamation started in 1992 and since then the height of Chek Lap Kok island has been reduced from 90 to 7 metres. The reclamation covers an area of 1248.5 hectares, an area as large as Kowloon peninsula, and will accommodate an airport terminal the size of London Heathrow and JFK New York put together.

The impact on the immediate surroundings is enormous. A new transport network of railways, highways, bridges and a cross-harbour tunnel is being built to support the airport. The North Lantau Expressway, two sections of Route 3 and the West Kowloon Expressway will be the major highways serving this new island. The Lantau Link comprises the 2.2-kilometre Tsing Ma bridge and a 500-metre viaduct linking it with a second shorter bridge. The 2-kilometre Western Harbour crossing connecting Central and West Kowloon will have six lanes and a maximum capacity of 180,000 vehicles a day. At Tung Chung, an area immediately opposite the airport island, a new town development is planned to accommodate over 200,000 people.

From over 30 international groups of architects and engineeers, eight were selected to tender and three were subsequently shortlisted. The contract for design of the passenger terminal was awarded to the Mott Consortium, of Mott Connell Limited, Foster Asia and BAA plc.

In its basic design concept, the building is not unlike Norman Foster's Stansted Airport, where a blanket of roof covers the entire terminal, unifying its various parts and functions and providing a symbolic identity. At Chek Lap Kok, over 120 lightweight structural shells (each spanning 36 metres and prefabricated in Singapore and the UK) were brought to the site and connected to form continuous barrel vaults running east–west

Future developments

Foster Asia (Hong Kong) Ltd 1992–

Future developments

Foster Asia (Hong Kong) Ltd 1992–

and give clear directions to the passengers below. The terminal building and aircraft gate spine will be almost 1.3 kilometres long.

All passengers will enter and leave the building through a vast entrance hall atrium, a meeting and greeting area for arrivals, while departing passengers will pass overhead on a number of glass-sided ramps. From the check-in area, departing passengers will pass through immigration and security control to a long concourse which runs west from the main body of the terminal before dividing into a 'Y'. An internal passenger train will link the east and west parts of the concourse.

In May 1996 the British and Chinese authorities agreed that the second (northern) runway could proceed earlier than originally planned. As a result the northern concourse of the terminal building will be expanded and extended to meet increased air traffic requirements. The concourse is designed to accommodate the new 'stretch' B747 600 passenger aircraft and other large aircraft of the future.

The airport will be capable of handling 35 million passengers in the first year, 1998, and, eventually, up to 87 million per annum.

Up to 3000 drawings have been produced by Foster and Partners since the beginning of the contract. AY

AIRPORT PLANNING, OPERATION ASPECTS AND SYSTEMS BAA plc
PROJECT MANAGEMENT, ENGINEERING INFRASTRUCTURE Mott Connell Limited
CONSTRUCTION, PROGRAMME & VALUE ENGINEERING O'Brien-Kreitzberg & Associates Ltd
QUANTITY SURVEYOR WT Partnership
SPECIALIST STRUCTURAL ENGINEERING Ove Arup & Partners
TRAFFIC ENGINEERING AND TRANSPORT PLANNING Wilbur Smith Assocs

Future developments

Foster Asia (Hong Kong) Ltd 1992–

Foster Asia (Hong Kong) Ltd 1992–

Chek Lap Kok: airport railway

Following the Hong Kong government's announcement in October 1989 of its intention to build Hong Kong's replacement airport at Chek Lap Kok off the north shore of Lantau Island, joint studies for a railway link were undertaken by the Mass Transit Railway Corporation and the government.

At present there are two MTR crossings between the Kowloon Peninsula and Hong Kong Island. This new rail link will be an extension of the existing MTR network. The expansion will provide two services – Lantau Line (a domestic mass transit service) and Airport Express – which will share running tracks over most of their routes. Lantau Line will link Central district and western Kowloon with Tsing Yi and Tung Chung on Lantau Island. The Airport Express, a dedicated high-speed service, will link Central and western Kowloon with Hong Kong's new international airport at Chek Lap Kok. Trains will operate at speeds of up to 135 kilometres an hour and will take 23 minutes from Central to the airport terminal building.

Five sites alongside the railway have been identified for massive property development. The land available at these sites totals approximately 62 hectares. The Hong Kong Central station will be built on reclaimed land in front of Exchange Square, with a subway connection to the existing MTR Central station. Three office towers and up to 1200 hotel rooms are to be built above the station.

The railway will continue underground, rising to an at-grade entry to Tai Kok Tsui station where only the Lantau Line service will stop. It will then continue at grade before rising on an elevated structure to Lai King. From Tsing Yi, the line will run in a tunnel before moving on to the Tsing Ma bridge, across Ma Wan Island and the Kap Shui Mun viaducts and then on to Lantau Island. The alignment will then go through Siu Ho Wan.

1998

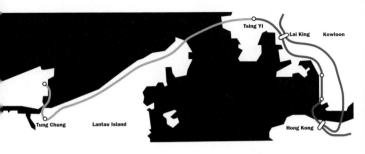

Tsing Yi

Lai King

Kowloon

Tung Chung

Lantau Island

Hong Kong

Future developments

1998

Lantau Line then proceeds to Tung Chung where 10,716 apartments will be built around the station. The last stop on the Airport Express Line will be at the airport terminal building.

MTRC anticipates that the final cost of the project will be within the estimated cost of HK$34 billion. The railway is scheduled for completion at the same time as the airport. AY

Future developments

1998

Hong Kong Convention and Exhibition Centre extension

As part of their efforts to reinforce Hong Kong as Asia's trade-fair capital, the Trade Development Council organised an international competition for an extension to the existing Hong Kong Convention and Exhibition Centre. At a packed press conference in September 1994, the Council's Chairman, Dr Victor Fung, unveiled the free-form expressive structure submitted by the Chicago-based international practice, Skidmore, Owings & Merrill, and a well-respected local office, Wong & Ouyang.

The architectural language of the new extension is completely different from that of the existing centre. A free-form metallic roof profile covers an 8500-square-metre column-free exhibition hall, connected at three levels to the existing building through a 75-metre link. There is also a fully glazed conference hall with 180-degree views of Victoria Harbour. Construction is taking place on 6.5 hectares of reclaimed land directly in front of the existing centre on the Wanchai waterfront, but separated from it by a 7.5-metre channel of water.

The extension, with 28,000 square metres of exhibition space and a 4500-seat conference hall, will more than double the usable space of the existing facility. It will also provide new transport links: a ferry pier serving cross-harbour routes; a direct link to Wanchai MTR station via covered footbridges; a public bus terminus; and two bridges connecting the site to Wanchai's road network and underground car parks. AY

LOCATION in front of Convention and Exhibition Centre, on the Wanchai waterfront
COST HK$3.4 billion
MTR Wanchai
ACCESS open

Future developments

SOM in association with Wong & Ouyang (Hong Kong) Ltd 1997–

Future developments

SOM in association with Wong & Ouyang (Hong Kong) Ltd 1997–

KCRC Kowloon station

The Hung Hom railway station was opened in the mid 1970s. At that time the rail link to China was one of the major construction projects in the city, along with the cross-harbour tunnel. Over the years the link grew in popularity until it finally reached a point where it could no longer meet the expectations of its daily commuters, tourists and business travellers. A series of additions and alterations carried out during the 1980s proved insufficient.

Foster Asia was appointed to tackle the problem, and 'double-decker' trains were introduced on the non-stop link to China in the late 1990s. KCRC Kowloon station will be extended to the east with a new lightweight pavilion which utilises the existing podium structure and foundation to create a concourse more than double the size of the current building. The lightweight 'wave' roof, incorporating rooflights and a full-height glazed curtain wall, will provide controlled natural daylight to all levels of the station. The platforms, public walkways and concourses will be linked by a series of atrium voids which penetrate through all levels of the building to allow natural daylight to reach the platforms below. The platform areas will be completely refurbished with improved lighting, signage, and floor and wall finishes.

Construction work began in 1995 and will be completed in a series of phases by early 1998. AY

ADDRESS 8 Cheong Wan Road, Hung Hom, Kowloon
SIZE 45,000 square metres
COST HK$1.3 billion

Future developments

Foster Asia 1995–8

Foster Asia 1995–8

Land reclamation

A sea of commercial towers rising up and dominating the mountains behind is the popular vision of Hong Kong and the progressive shifting of the shoreline reinforces this impression. Continuous urban expansion, due to rapid economic growth in the Pearl River delta and other parts of south China, has created bands of reclamation along the northern foreshore of the island and Kowloon peninsula, as well as on neighbouring islands.

Central/Wanchai

The proposed business centre expansion on 1.28 square kilometres of reclaimed land will generate up to 3 million square metres of commercial, residential and community-related uses, together with major areas of public open space and interconnected malls, arcades and pedestrian promenades along a 3-kilometre stretch of the northern foreshore on Hong Kong Island. In addition, more than 30 hectares of existing waterfront sites are to be redeveloped as part of a co-ordinated programme. The scheme is currently being implemented, with an extended planning horizon of 2011.

West Kowloon

The West Kowloon reclamation is an Airport Core Project. The feasibility of extending the reclamation to the Kowloon Point area, and the opportunities this will present for a fully integrated new waterfront as a focus for tourist activities, is currently being studied.

A framework to guide the planning and development of West Kowloon up to the year 2011 has been formulated on the basis of the upgrading, comprehensive redevelopment and thinning out of the older areas, together with development on new reclamation. The project will create

much-needed open space and community facilities, and housing/relocation sites for development.

South-east Kowloon

The overall objective is to restructure the existing Kai Tak airport site, including the improvement of adjoining areas of obsolete housing. A fundamental factor underlying the masterplan has been the need to create a 'city within a city'. Landscape provides the structure of the new area, with a central park of 78 hectares, major urban squares and pedestrian corridors.

Guidelines have been developed for each of the seven planning areas on the proposed reclamation to emphasise its particular role. Each would be within walking distance of an MTR or light railway station. The masterplan includes a commercial, residential and urban complex on the new waterfront; an educational, cultural and business complex on the old airport apron; and residential areas to meet different sectors of demand. It provides for a planned population of 285,000 people and 110,000 jobs.

Lantau Port development

Hong Kong port is a critical part of the territory's infrastructure. Its industrial and commercial business provides employment for 350,000 people. Although it is already the world's busiest container port, a completely new port with twice the capacity of the present facilities is needed to meet forecast growth in demand. The creation of a new port would involve reclaiming enough land to add 1 per cent to the total land area of Hong Kong.

Planning for this massive task began in the mid 1980s when it became clear that the container port would have to be expanded and the existing

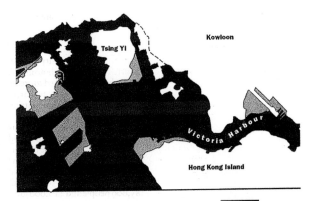

Committed Reclamation

Proposed Reclamation

Future developments

airport replaced. In October 1989, the Governor announced that the new airport and container port would be built on Lantau Island, sharing common infrastructure and communication facilities. The phased development of a new port at North Lantau will provide up to a further 24 berths and 4700 hectares of anchorage space, mostly to the west of Hong Kong Island and between Lamma Island and Cheung Chau. AY

Index

Hong Kong: a guide to recent architecture

Hong Kong: a guide to recent architecture

Hong Kong: a guide to recent architecture

Hong Kong: a guide to recent architecture